BDSM Mastery—Basics your guide to play, parties, and scene protocols

by Robert J. Rubel Ph.D.
and
M. Jen Fairfield

BDSM Mastery—Basics your guide to play, parties, and scene protocols

by Robert J. Rubel Ph.D.
and
M. Jen Fairfield

BDSM Mastery—Basics your guide to play, parties, and scene protocols

by Robert J. Rubel Ph.D.
and
M. Jen Fairfield

Red 8 Ball Press

www.KinkMastery.com

Red Eight Ball Press
P.O. Box 171303
Austin, TX 78717

BDSM Mastery—Basics:
Your guide to play, parties, and scene protocols
© 2014 by Robert J. Rubel and M. Jen Fairfield

ISBN: 978-0-9863521-0-2

Cover Design: M. Jen Fairfield and RhodesCreativeStudio
Cover Photo: iStock

Library of Congress Catalog Number: 2014959194

Published by Red Eight Ball Press
Printed in the United States of America

Dedicated to the brave, kinky explorers
who pass on what they have learned
so that we who follow them
can explore even further.

Dear Readers -

There are two troubling aftereffects that arise when I write a book. Actually, these aftereffects arise when anyone in our BDSM community writes a book.

First, some readers will read only part of the book, focus on points they object to, and then speak widely about how this writer doesn't have a clue about how things are really done rather than read through the material with an eye to adapting concepts and ideas that speak to them.

Second, written words lock an author's thoughts into place in peoples' minds. Authors get associated with certain viewpoints and it can be challenging to get previous readers to understand that an author has broadened their under- standing of a topic over the span of years.

This second point is important, for reading a book is rather like looking at a snapshot: this is a slice of material representing our viewpoints at this time. The same photographer/writer working with similar material five years into the future will produce a different image or book. That's understandable, as they've learned more over time.

I have learned a great deal about BDSM and Master/ slave material since my last books in the 2006-7 period. I hope you enjoy the differences.

— *Robert J. (Dr. Bob) Rubel*

Acknowledgments

There are a select few other people who have gone out of their way to help make this book what it has become and I owe each of them a deep debt of gratitude:

- david stein (david_stein on Fet) inspired me to make this book more broad and complete than originally intended and then guided me heavily in the book's organization. His comments and edits—particularly on the first chapter—have substantially improved this work. david's deep knowledge of this field and no-nonsense approach to writing has been a true blessing.

- PhoenixRed (her scene name on Fet) holds a Ph.D. both in Psychology and in Neural Science and has been active in the local Kansas City area BDSM community since 2006. She has poured her heart and soul into two complete readings of this book, once to make substantive comments and once to conduct a complete editorial review. This is no trivial matter, and I am grateful beyond words for the breadth of experience and balance she has brought to this work. Thanks, Phoenix, you've made a difference.

- Sir_Dragon_Z (his name on Fet, from Victoria, B.C., Canada) was one of the final readers. His thoughtful comments about D/s relationships helped make a number of important sections of this book far richer than they would otherwise have been. Outgoing and gregarious, Sir Dragon's subtle observations frequently surprise me. Even while standing and speaking with him, I frequently find myself reaching for my notebook in order to capture his ideas. "Wait, wait," I'll say, "What did you just say?" Thanks B., you're a gem!

Other Books by Robert J. Rubel and M. Jen Fairfield

Books are published by Red Eight Ball Press, Austin, TX and are available through www.KinkMastery.com or through Amazon.

BDSM Mastery—Relationships: a guide for creating mindful relationships for Dominants and submissives
(Book Two in the BDSM Mastery Series)

Master/slave Mastery: Updated handbook of concepts, approaches, and practices
(Book One in the Master/slave Mastery Series)

Master/slave Mastery: Refining the fire—ideas that matter
(Book Two in the Master/slave Mastery Series)

Is THAT what they meant? A book of practical communication insights

Preface

Since discovering the world of BDSM in 2001, I've spent a lot of time reading, writing, and thinking about this culture. As interest in BDSM has recently exploded, books and websites have sprung up offering countless of thousands of facts and opinions about it. Some of this material is superb, but other material wanders between "sort of right but too superficial" through the land of "maybe, but not in my experience" to the quicksand of "who in the world made this up."

My Ph.D. is in educational sociology; since 2006, I've been writing books and doing demos and presentations at BDSM conferences worldwide. I've led well over 200 classes and workshops, and since Fall 2012, my co-author and I have been conducting free hour-long twice- monthly webinars on various BDSM topics. Over this time, I've learned to identify when BDSM material is generally accurate or a little *off*.

I wrote this book to help you safely cross the bridge from personal curiosity to the real worlds of kink and also as a kind of "decoding manual" for BDSMers who have come to realize how complex and confusing this world can be.

By the time you finish this book, you'll know what to expect and how to behave in...

"Everyone in BDSM starts at the same place. Where they end up is a function of their interests and the choices they make along the way."

— *Mindi*, my former slave of eight years

- a *munch*—an informal gathering of people interested in BDSM, usually held at a restaurant;
- a BDSM club meeting—often where you'll find informative presentations about the scene; and
- a *play party*—a private or semi-public event where devotees of various sadomasochistic (SM) and other kinky activities engage with complementary partners.

Most importantly, you'll be able to identify suitable partners for safely participating in these activities.

I had three guiding principles in writing this book: First, to present the material in a way that honors the intent behind the slogan that BDSM is "safe, sane, and consensual." Second, to communicate that BDSM is about creating and having memorable experiences. Third, to stress that safe SM play requires training and practice.

This book specifically does **not** cover two areas: Details about how to perform particular SM skills and discussions about forming BDSM-based relationships. Supplement C lists some truly outstanding how-to books; relationship material is addressed in a separate book: *BDSM Mastery—Relationships: guide for creating mindful relationships for Dominants and submissives* Robert J. Rubel, Ph.D. and M. Jen Fairfield. (Book Two in the BDSM Mastery Series).

I've included an extensive glossary of BDSM terms in Supplement A. You might want to scan over it before you begin reading the book; it will help you understand words and phrases that are not part of your usual vocabulary.

Some notes about writing style

I write in first person present tense so that I can speak with you directly (I dislike academic prose). Also, I write in spirals, so if you think you've already heard me say "X," chances are you did. I do this in order to lay down one layer of ideas upon which I can then add other layers of more complex ideas.

I follow the common BDSM writing convention of referring to people who are filling the role of the submissive partner as a "sub" and if a personal name of a sub is to be mentioned, the first letter of that sub's name will be in lowercase. However, I make no assumption that a sub is either male or female, for gender has very little to do with where one falls on the scale of dominance-submission.

Carrying this thought a bit further, I've endeavored to keep this book gender-neutral. Rather than "Dom," I write it as "Dom/me"—a combination of the abbreviation for a male dominant (Dom) and a female dominant (Domme, pronounced the same as Dom). Also, as bottoms (those on the receiving end of BDSM play) may be either male or female, I avoid referring to them as "subs" or "she," favoring "they" or "them," as in: "The Dom/me may instruct them to do X," rather than saying, "The Dom may instruct her to do X."

I'm writing this way because very little in the world of BDSM actually depends on gender or sexual orientation and I'm endeavoring to break you right now of some cultural habits that can get you in trouble in this world. People usually assume that Doms are male and submissives are female. It's not that clean-cut in reality.

Personal biases that influence my writing

I have some personal biases you should be aware of.

I am pro-women and anti-macho and pro-learning/practice and anti- improvisation. While it can be lots of fun to play Tarzan and Jane during a scene (hope you're not too young to get that reference), I'm concerned that—in the excitement of their newly discovered world—Tarzan may overlook some of Jane's needs for support and encouragement in the non-BDSM parts of their lives.

I believe that it's important for Tarzan's and Jane's BDSM activities to augment their sexual and intellectual growth. Otherwise they risk reinforcing a stereotype of male-Dominant BDSM: "Me Tarzan, Jane my property! Jane do as me say or me beat Jane!" Oh, and a safety tip for Tarzan: Be sure your rope is secured correctly before trying to swing into our community.

Once you "swing in," you're going to find BDSM a world of mind-bending combinations and contradictions. This book, the first in the *BDSM Mastery* series, is intended to demystify this world without draining any of the excitement.

About my co-author

Despite the book's first-person-singular style, M. Jen Fairfield influenced virtually every section either directly or indirectly. I could not have written it without her constant influence in my life. That is why she is listed as co-author: She earned the position.

For those who are curious—and particularly those who see us at conferences—I'll say up front that Jen is 20 years younger than me and had no prior BDSM experience before we began dating in March 2010. However, during our years together, her continual questions, her probing, and her wide-ranging kinky interests have spurred me to do more and more research about BDSM—in part to satisfy her nearly insatiable mind.

Thanks to Jen's influence in my life, *BDSM Mastery* is quite different from my previous books on Master/slave relationships. Born in 1944, I grew up during the height of the Cold War, when John F. Kennedy was President and my father worked as a senior official at the Pentagon. Jen was born during the Kennedy administration and came of age as a hippie. My earlier books lack her influence, and those who have read (or will read) them will be struck by that difference.

Perhaps the best reason why Jen is credited as the co-author is that the book simply wouldn't have taken the same shape, texture, or tone without her.

Oh—one last thought: *please be patient*, both in BDSM and in reading this book. Rushing blindly into new situations rarely ends well. Even if your eyes glaze over reading pages in which I carefully analyze key terms and concepts, sooner or later you'll find every bit of this book relevant to finding your way in the BDSM world, where little details can quickly become *big* issues.

— *Robert J. Rubel*, Austin, Texas 2014

Table of Contents

Introduction
What *is* BDSM anyway?

This is not a book that explains what BDSM *is*, this is a book that explains what BDSM *is all about*.

The letters "BDSM" represent an open-ended range of practices and expressions—including many forms of restraint, sensory stimulation, role- playing, and interpersonal dynamics. These activities are usually erotic at some level, but might not involve genital intercourse. "BDSM" derives from a combination of the letters "B&D," for bondage and discipline (corporal punishment), and "S&M" (also "S/M" or "SM") for sadism and masochism (or sado-masochism), which typically involves pain and/ or humiliation. It was later noticed that the letters "D&S" in the

"i am an active lifestyle participant in BDSM. It is not a lifestyle for everyone, and not everyone who is a part of the lifestyle necessarily participates in a 24/7 BDSM life. Some people save it just for the weekends, or even just once a month."

— *kerin*, Yahoo Answers

middle can stand for Dominance and submission (D/s). Since both B&D and SM usually involve at least temporary dominance by one person over another who submits to the former's control, most people in the BDSM world these days view it as a kind of three-ring circus where participants can either move around or stay focused on just one or two rings.

For some, BDSM is about authority-based relationships—the giving or receiving of service that may or may not be sexual. For others, BDSM is about intensifying their sexual relations. For still others, BDSM is about losing themselves temporarily in intense sensations or unusual psychological (or even spiritual) states resulting from bondage or pain play. Of course, there are also the edgy few who are drawn to pain-centered SM practices simply *because* they are taboo within the mainstream culture. Moths to flames, as it were.

Historical origins of BDSM

The historical origins of SM and B&D as erotic practices are obscure. Researchers have found examples of SM as far back as the 6th century BCE at an Etruscan burial site in what is now part of Italy; an erotic depiction of two men striking a woman with a cane was found inside a burial chamber. You could also have a look at India's famed *Kama Sutra* (written between 400 BCE and 200 CE) to fin explicit descriptions of different ways to strike your partner during sex. It tells where to hit, and even describes some of the "joyful cries of pain" the strikes evoke. It also says that impact play, biting, and pinching during sex require the woman's consent since not everyone enjoys pain of this sort, making it one of the first written guides to SM techniques and safety.

Some historians propose that SM emerged as a distinct form of sexual behavior at the beginning of the 18th century as medical and legal professionals began categorizing human sexuality in an effort to understand it. Slowly, these activities began appearing in novels like *Fanny Hill* (1749). As early as 1769, there are reports of London brothels specializing in flogging, *the English vice.*

The terms *sadism* and *masochism* derive from the names of two infamous erotic writers, the Marquis de Sade and Leopold von Sacher- Masoch, respectively. Sade's descriptions are more comparable to snuff stories and movies than to our modern BDSM practices that stress safety and informed consent. Sacher-Masoch's novel *Venus in Furs* is much less about pain than about Dominant/submissive relationships; the woman is the Dominant.

The dance of intimacy

For those who use BDSM for sexual purposes, mastering SM techniques has the surprising capacity to transform mundane sexual experiences into something quite extraordinary—what I call *connected sex*. That is, SM play practices (when done safely/correctly and with the right intent) can lead directly to an intimate *connection* between partners. As a **bottom**, you will begin to experience connected sex once you play with someone who has mastered a range of SM skills *and* has also learned how to select from among those skills and apply them with greater or lesser intensity in response to your own reactions. As a **Top**, once you learn how to correctly combine SM and erotic stimulation to the degree and extent that builds the bottom's stimulation and pleasure, you will develop the capacity to leave your partner shaking and vibrating from an unforgettable orgasm.

BDSM sex is often both more complex and more intimate than conventional— or *plain vanilla*—sex (especially the kind depicted in most porn videos); it involves discovering and mastering broad, sophisticated, and often counterintuitive

Connection during sex

Connected sex occurs when the Top (the person controlling the action) has mastered both a range of SM skills and the ability to read the emotions/reactions of the bottom (the person being acted upon). If all goes right, the Top can leave the bottom shaking and vibrating from an unforgettable orgasm.

ways of playing and connecting with your partner. It is possible to create a remarkably potent experience of sexual connection by combining components of a D/s *relationship* (service, protocols, and discipline) and SM *play* (carefully administered intense sensations) with established sex practices (fucking, fingering, licking). The psychological "control-and-surrender" interplay between people in a power- imbalanced (Dominant/submissive) relationship that's enhanced by competent SM play can create nights or even mere moments you will remember all your life.

BDSM's darker side

As you may hear in public discussions about BDSM, there is a dark side, too. Some people are drawn to BDSM hoping somehow to heal or desensitize past hurts and to find love and trust. Others hope they can construct loving and emotionally close families to replace their dysfunctional or failed biological families. While some are able to heal and find the love and personal comfort that they seek, logic tells us that others will end up in BDSM relationships that are not good for them, and that a few will end up in relationships that repeatedly trigger past traumas even though the individuals involved may not understand how or why.

This is not the place to discuss BDSMers who may have experienced past psychological trauma, but it *is* the place to mention that choosing to participate in this way of life is a decision to be transformed in some way. While most people who take the (substantial) step to explore BDSM find others who are easy to get along

"Just because you are a Dominant doesn't mean you are hurting a woman. I personally find submissive women to be much better treated in the BDSM community than in most. Any guy lucky enough to have one knows she's a treasure and treats and respects her as such."

— *Want2TieMeUp*, Yahoo Answers

with socially and psychologically, others do not. Some people who start down the BDSM path ultimately conclude that it's not a good path for them. As they learn more about themselves, they realize that their initial reasons for participating in unusual relationship structures or in edgy forms of sexuality are not necessarily good reasons. In fact, some will discover that their participation in BDSM has made them more wary, less trusting, and more isolated than they were before they started. So please be aware that while many who enter here find a welcome home, others do not.

This brings up another controversial topic. Some people seem to think they can heal past traumas through BDSM rather than through professional therapy. This is not a great idea and can easily backfire. Your experience of the BDSM community—and your success at being a good partner for someone else—benefits from starting out emotionally strong and healthy as well as from knowing something of your own motivations and drives. Such self-knowledge can take a lot of thought and work: swimming successfully in the BDSM waters requires you to wake up and pay attention. You can hurt someone or be hurt by someone both physically and emotionally. This is an alternative way of living your life, not a game.

As you will discover throughout this book, *communication* and *trust* are core elements of BDSM relationships. Whether short- or long-term, successful BDSM relationships are based on clear and honest communication. This is particularly important, because much of what goes on between partners in this lifestyle can be edgy. Trust between partners quiets the natural fear of new experiences and helps both the Top and the bottom to release emotionally and relax into the relationship dynamic or their SM play.

BDSM and the Internet

The Internet brought a wealth of opportunities. Not only did it provide a way to find like-minded people worldwide, but it also enabled previously isolated groups to share their ideas. As the Internet evolved, LGBT communities, SM and Leather communities, and swinger communities all gained a forum. People

"I'm a newbie in this world, but I've come to realize that without communication and trust, you can't get anywhere in your relationship—whatever format it may be. My Dom and I have had scenes that have fallen short of expectations on either side due to poor negotiation and a lack of honest communication as well as of the trust required to be honest with each other."

— *Pryia*, a beta reader of this book

who liked rope bondage, electrical stimulation, or erotic photography could find one another. Best of all, it provided a way for people to communicate anonymously with one another to discuss ideas that had largely been hidden and taboo throughout history.

This rich mixture of people and ideas helped create an explosion of interest in (and knowledge about) BDSM that continues to this day. As the Internet brought people together, it also helped trigger a tremendous growth of BDSM clubs in cities across the U.S. and around the world. Some clubs formed around people with a specific sexual orientation (gay, lesbian, trans-gendered, etc.) while other clubs welcomed people of any sexual persuasion (pansexual clubs). Some clubs formed around SM interests (whip clubs, rope clubs), and some clubs formed around relationship interests (Dom clubs, FemDomme clubs, Master/slave clubs).

Nowadays, the Internet provides a central platform for networking among those of us interested in things kinky. Since 2008, we have even had our own social-networking site. FetLife.com is the BDSMers version of Facebook.

Vanilla vs. BDSM

"Vanilla sex" is the term that BDSM aficionados use to mean intercourse-related play without the kinky stuff such as bondage,

SM sensations, or power-imbalanced relationship dynamics. Vanilla sex is not limited to missionary-position heterosexual intercourse, but includes about anything you'd see in a standard gay or straight porn movie—oral sex, anal sex, plus an ass-slapping or two. While vanilla sex can be lots of fun (even for kinksters, some of us have found more interesting ways to play sexually. Actually, from the BDSM point of view, vanillas are *restricting* themselves to that flavor of sex, whether out of principle, personal sexual preference, or lack of knowledge about the alternatives. *Vanilla* is not a pejorative term, simply a descriptor.

Obviously, a good many vanilla folks like to spice up their sex lives occasionally with playful spankings or even light bondage (silk scarves or neckties). But unlike BDSM practitioners, vanillas don't *purposefully* use SM pain play or D/s power exchange to heighten their partners' erotic or emotional state. In BDSM, arousal techniques may involve some mix of...

- toys (from vibrators and dildos to floggers, canes, electrical gear, piercing needles, and much more);
- SM techniques (knowing where, how, and in what order to use the equipment—including your hands or genitals);
- assumed roles (such as Teacher/student, Lord/Lady or Lord/lackey, Master/slave, Owner/pet, Daddy/little, and so on); or
- psychological dynamics of power exchange, authority transfer, hypnosis, etc.

In BDSM play, you may find a Top who takes 30 minutes or more to beautifully and artistically bind a bottom in elaborate rope designs that suspends them a few feet off the ground. There will only be sex if it was negotiated previously. *Rope* is their kink, intercourse is the afterthought.

In BDSM play, what you see may not be what is actually going on. This is not the vanilla world of WYSIWYG (**W**hat **Y**ou **S**ee **I**s **W**hat **Y**ou **G**et). Here, you may find a heterosexual couple dressed in fetish outfit dining at a table set with crystal and bone china. It looks eccentric but still almost vanilla—except that the

"Subspace," you say?

"The next level is sometimes called 'blonde space.' This is probably the first part of subspace I experience. I forget commands, look spacey, and do not respond to anything I am told. I drop things. I do not speak; I can't. I giggle a lot, and sometimes I will cry. If asked if anything is bothering me, I wouldn't be able to say— as I really would not know. Sometimes, I babble in a language only I understand. I could not use a safeword even if I tried. I need to know that the Dominant will look after me."

— *Pryia*

woman has a bipolar chrome electrical probe inserted into her vagina, and the man has the power control next to his dinner plate. He turns up the power every so often, sending muscle-contracting spasms throughout her groin; she screams. Then she giggles like mad after absorbing the intense sensations. She thinks this is fun and funny. She's kinky. She's my partner.

As you learn more about BDSM, you'll hear more about **good pain** and **bad pain.** What was just described is an example of good pain, and the scene just described is definitely **not vanilla.**

BDSM sexual play also differs from vanilla sexual play because the SM activities often act as emotional intensifiers. If you think that you had a spectacular bonding experience the first time you had sex with the love of your life, what you'll experience with a skilled BDSM partner will rock your world. A woman's first experience of blasting off into *subspace* often leaves them astonished and addicted to these utterly new and foreign sensations. (I often respond to questions related to this topic in my "experts" role on www. allexperts.com.)

Tools and work vs. toys and play

In the U.S., a large cadre of the straight BDSM community refers to the equipment we use to augment sex play as *toys*. This includes everything you can think of: vibrators, floggers, paddles, whips, and so on. However, another large cadre of the BDSM community refers to these same implements as *tools*. In fact, the group that refers to them as *tools* were already using this equipment by the time vanillas began developing an interest in rough sex.

More than that, people who use the word *toys*, use those toys to *play* with their bottom; people who use the word *tools* uses those tools to *work* with their bottom. As words communicate concepts, saying that you will set out *toys* for a *play session* communicates a different message than if you said you will set out *tools* for a *work* session. Those who use the words *toys* and *play* and the words *tools* and *work* come from different subcultures within BDSM. Since most readers belong to the *toys* and *play* community, I'll use those words in this book.

Separating activity from authority roles

I've taken care throughout this book to distinguish *activity roles* from *authority roles*. In the way I've come to understand the world of BDSM, *activity* roles concern whether someone is giving sensations (Top) or receiving sensations (bottom) whereas *authority roles* concern whether someone is giving orders (Dominant) or following orders (submissive).

While these distinctions apply best to what happens in a play session (a *scene*), some couples discover that because the roles actually express their personalities, they build real-time relationships around them (e.g., Master/slave and Owner/pet). I cover this aspect of BDSM in my companion book: *BDSM Mastery—Relationships: a guide for creating mindful relationships for Dominants and submissives* by Robert J. Rubel, Ph.D. and M. Jen Fairfield (Book Two in the BDSM Mastery Series). There was just too much material to include it all in this book—and, anyway, not everyone enters the BDSM world to become involved in a relationship.

Chapter 1
A Thousand Questions

> "Why should I become
> involved with BDSM? Is it
> safe? How do I meet people?
> How in the world do I *start*?

For Tops (those *doing* the action), this book is intended to offer you the wisdom to know how to proceed ethically in our community; for bottoms (those *receiving* the action), this book is intended to offer you the knowledge about how to play safely.

If you've bought this book, I suspect that you already realize that there is a lot going on in a culture that you only recently knew existed. Also, you probably have some sense that you're at the front-end of a personal project called: "I'm interested in having a great experience with BDSM," and you're feeling a little overwhelmed.

This chapter is intended to help you to understand the BDSM culture, whom you're likely to meet in that world, and what BDSM can mean for you, personally.

Why become involved with BDSM?

As you're reading this book, I think you are ready and willing to learn a lot about BDSM and its relation to your everyday life, so let's get started. Here are some of the more common reasons people have for entering this culture.

It's fun and exciting and sexy and so taboo. The very fact that the public press makes such a fuss out of sex and sexually-different people is enough to get many people to start asking questions on their own.

It's comforting to know that I'm not so weird. Some people feel that they just don't fit in with their peers. They suspect that their sexual interests and dark fantasies might be a little unusual or extreme. In BDSM, these same people find that others have similar or even more extreme sexual preferences. They find friends.

I just can't get these sensations anywhere else—not safely. For many folks, BDSM provides opportunities to have experiences they can't get anywhere else. After all, where else could you go to find someone who will play with live fire over your body? Where else can you go to find someone with a passion for forced orgasms? Who do you know who can leave you vibrating after sex, unable to walk for 20–30 minutes? Where else can you find someone who will make pretty patterns on your skin with hypodermic needles?

I want to stretch my imagination. Many walk the BDSM path in order to stretch their imaginations in the bedroom. In your bedroom, you can be whomever you wish—torturer or obedient slave, vamp or Sleeping Beauty. You can make your partner beg for mercy or enjoy begging yourself. With some imagination and effort, you can rearrange or redecorate your bedroom/apartment/ house to support your wildest fantasies. Here, you can cross the line from what you've been experiencing in your sex life to what you've been *fantasizing about having* in your sex life. Living in the world of BDSM makes it fun to take charge—or to surrender.

The people I meet and the sex I have are just so boring. BDSM lets us try out our fantasies to decide whether we like them enough to try them again, and by playing different roles, we can determine our own sexual proclivities; if done right—thoughtfully and with intent and integrity— you'll be able to craft yourself an entirely new life. BDSM can transform you. Where else can we experiment with rough and unusual sex practices without seeming odd or weird than in a BDSM gathering? Where else can you offer yourself as a gift to another person knowing that they can't make the magic happen without your consent and willingness? Being in a relationship where you trust another person to be responsible for what happens to you is an amazing gift, and *trust* is the key.

And, yes, magic **can** happen once you firmly establish that bond of trust. You can let go without losing yourself. You can put your fears, anxieties, and even your orgasms in the hands of another... who then makes the decisions about what your body will and will not experience. You can enter an alternate universe.

But it's a one-way door you're thinking of walking through. Very few can go back to vanilla. It will change your worldview and your sexual preferences forever.

As a bottom, you will experience incredibly heightened sensations. You will become hyper-aware of every inch of your body once you realize that you're unable to control what happens to you. It's an amazing and

Fear as an aphrodisiac

"Fear triggers the fight-or-flight response, fueled by adrenaline, which, as it turns out, is chemically related to amphetamines. Granted, it's a very different kind of high for mindfuckers: not a mellow, floaty 'my vulva is one with the universe' high but a jittery, revved-up 'oh fuck oh fuck oh fuck' kind of high. Endorphins are like great downers, but adrenaline is uppers all the way. And it's just as addictive. Don't believe me? Go ask anyone who likes to bungee jump or skydive."

— *Edge*, from "Mindfuck" in The Ultimate Guide to Kink, ed. Tristan Taormino (Cleis, 2012)

13

addictive experience. We've all heard the old adage, "There's a fine line between pleasure and pain." A skilled Top can enable you to ride that fine line and take you to greater heights than you've previously imagined.

Discovering who you are

People often start out in the world of BDSM with a rather fuzzy understanding of who they are and what they want. In fact, much of the fun of exploring this world comes from watching yourself grow, develop, and bloom into a person you did not know was inside you.

This line of thought raises an interesting and relevant question: *How were you guided to become the person you are?* Think back to when you were a teenager and started dating. What kind of advice did your parents give you? What kind of advice did you give your own kids?

- Play nicely with others and be a nice person.
- Respect your elders.
- Find nice friends.
- Do well in school and stay in school until you graduate.
- Be polite and well spoken; use nice table manners.
- You're only as good as your word.
- Do unto others as you would have others do unto you.
- And so on, right?

There's nothing wrong with such maxims—you recognize them and know many more. But, here's where I'm going with this: my guess is that when your personality was forming in adolescence, nobody suggested that you look into yourself and try to figure out...

- whether you were a Dominant, a submissive, or a switch (someone who sometimes identifies as a Dominant and other times as a submissive);

- whether you were a masochist or a sadist, a Top or bottom;
- whether you liked pain, and under what conditions; or
- whether you liked being spanked, teased, or tied up, or preferred doing that to others.

I promise that you'll learn more about yourself as you gain experience in this culture. But not everyone can be neatly classified as a *Dom* (male Dominant), *Domme* (female Dominant) or *sub* (submissive of either gender). Not only are such traits influenced by cultural rules and by a person's upbringing, but the way people present themselves is contextual—what is going on around people influences both how they behave *and* how they are perceived by others:

- What is intended as politeness may be taken by some as submission.
- A wary submissive may give off signals of dominance as a form of emotional self-defense.
- Normally laid-back and mild-mannered people can become aggressively dominant when they perceive a threat to a loved one.

Who one is can take some thinking. Here's an example: A friend of mine on FetLife (SnowFlock), wrote me about the confusion she was experiencing as she tried to figure out who she is in order to explain herself to potential partners. With her permission, I'm including most of her message here:

Snow, as she is called in person, wrote: "So far, I know the following about me:

- "I'm not sure where exactly I fit in relation to roles—Domme/ Top, sub/bottom—so I identify as a *switch.*
- "I definitely have dominance in my personality, but I don't know if I'm a full Domme.
- "I have a sadistic side for sure, but I prefer to focus more on what a boy *does* for me in the realm of service.
- "I *love* having 'service'-type boys, as I'm not a service-type

or "domesticated" kind of woman.

- "I don't want to have to make all the decisions. Even if I had a boy, I would ask if he wants to do *xyz* versus telling him that we are now going to do *xyz*.

- "I can casually dominate someone, but I cannot casually submit to them, as "submitting"—at least to me—involves *emotional attachment* and a much greater chance of getting deeply hurt.

- "I dominate without sex as none of the boys that I've yet met have demonstrated a long-term serious commitment where I wanted to have sex. Sex would have to be within a committed relationship.

- "I am very open to various BDSM activities as long as there is no sex. These can be casual or even short-term relationships.

- "I am a masochist for sure, and when it comes to sex/bedroom, I'm more of a follower (submissive) sexually than a leader, yet outside of the bedroom/sex I'm very assertive.

- "As a sub, I can give up *some* (not all) control in a relationship for fun and play, but *don't* try to control me 24/7 or I will withdraw or put up a fight/argument.

- "As a sub, I'm less into service and control, though that changes depending on how deeply in love I am and how much I want to please Him [my Dom]. I'm definitely into activities such as bondage, spanking, flogging, etc.

Snow came to some truly valuable insights that then helped her describe her needs to a potential partner. Continuing with her quoted material:

- "A relationship doesn't have to involve the *usual* or *expected* Dom/sub roles—you can have other configurations or descriptors for the roles.

- "To play the Dom/me or sub in a scene, you don't need to have the matching Dominant or a submissive *personality* per se. The two people could play whatever roles they feel would be fun.

- "A Dom/me doesn't necessarily need to be a sadist, but could be a masochist. A sub doesn't necessarily need to be a masochist, but could even be a sadist or be more into service or even more focused on the play aspect of BDSM."

Snow realized that whether you're Dominant or submissive, you should know what makes you tick. A woman might say, "I like to serve, but I don't like to be told what to do." A man might say, "I make decisions all day long and don't want to be asked my opinion when I get home; just tell me what to do." Someone else might say, "In general, I'm a Dominant, but I occasionally find a person to whom I could submit.

As I've said repeatedly, you can reinvent yourself within the BDSM world. But few people do, either because it hadn't occurred to them that they could or because it seemed too much work. Remember this, though: As you enter the BDSM world, nobody knows the "old you" unless you tell them. Once you're here, fellow BDSMers are much more understanding if you decide to explore hidden sides of yourself. You can release the Dominant or submissive or Daddy/Mommy or little boy/girl within you and your BDSM friends will still be your friends. At least that's how it's supposed to work.

Before you begin to explore the role(s) you'll play in this culture, I urge you to take the time to understand their subtleties. Regardless of how others define them, the important part is how *you and your partners* define these words/roles within your specific relationships. (This *relationship* material is covered in depth in the companion book: *BDSM Mastery—Relationships: a guide for creating mindful relationships for Dominants and submissives* by Robert J. Rubel, Ph.D. and M. Jen Fairfield (Book Two in the BDSM Mastery Series).

If you aren't completely happy with yourself, you have the opportunity to change yourself so that you are happier; you *can* find what you're looking for, maybe even before you're sure you know what it is.

Scene names and titles

Unless you fear repercussions from friends, family, or work, you *can* use your legal name in the BDSM world. However, you probably should consider adopting a different name if you *are* worried about people connecting you to BDSM. Please be aware: It's not uncommon for children to be taken away from their custodial Parent just because they participate in BDSM. I personally know of a number of such cases.

For submissives: If you enter into a power-imbalanced relationship (e.g., Dominant/submissive or Master/slave), your Dom/me may wish to rename you as part of the power exchange. Your new name becomes a constant reminder that this is not a vanilla relationship.

Pick a practical scene name

It can be a challenge to find a name for your sub or slave (often collectively referred to as an *s-type*) that is sufficiently evocative yet also acceptable for public use. While you might enjoy calling your s-type *slut* or *cunt* in private, it won't work when you're out shopping or at a restaurant.

Doms and Masters may wish to be equally cautious about the scene names they select, as some may stick in the craw of other Dominants— or just seem silly to those more established in the scene. If George picks "Dom George" (or if Tasha picks "Goddess Maria") as a scene name, it can seem pretentious or insecure (it's almost like giving oneself a title as a way of forcing others to recognize one's desired status). And even more colorful choices, like

---

If you're going to use a scene name, pick one that can be called out in public. You're not going to want to shout, "Hey, Twinkle Toes!" in the middle of a grocery store. And you're certainly not going to want "Twinkle Toes" to shout back, "Over here, Grand Whipman!"

"Big Man" or "Master Full," risk drawing unfavorable attention. As you are selecting a scene name, consider how *you* would react to that name if someone were introduced that way to you.

Most often, folks choose a scene name that is a common given name, just not their own. Thus, "Mike" is really Bill, and "Cynthia" is really Mary. I've known some people for many years and have been surprised to discover that the name I've been using for them all that time is really a scene name.

Some names for submissive women are more, um, *appropriate* than others:

- Names like "Cat," "Kitten," and "Scarlet" can pass pretty much anywhere, for people recognize these as names;

- Names like "Babygirl," "Hot Stuff," and "Angelpie" can pass in most settings, as people will recognize them as endearments used within an established relationship. (However, you may run into trouble introducing your girl in a business setting or to your family. "Mr. Collins, I'd like you to meet Hot Stuff" may not help him think of you as executive material.); and

- Names like "Pussy," "Succulence," "Curious," "Pixie Doodle," and "Chocolate Hussy" are going to stop traffic if you're overheard using them in public. (An opening such as: "Hi, Mr. Collins, I'd like you to meet Pixie Doodle" can suck the air out of a room.)

I certainly don't mean to criticize anyone for the names they select; often it's the Dominant partner who chooses it. Just evaluate any name you consider in light of its impact on the public and on others in the community. Remember: BDSM is about consent. Inflicting your personal fetishes in public (including off-putting scene names) is non- consensual so far as the vanillas are concerned.

Personally, I learned this lesson the hard way. My slave's first scene name was *luscious*. It lasted until we went grocery shopping. I wanted to call to her as she was walking away down an aisle, but with other people nearby, I just couldn't bring myself to shout, "Luscious, while you're getting the milk, grab some sharp cheddar, please." I renamed her on the drive home.

Titles—self-assumed or earned?

Titles in the BDSM world can be controversial, and I'm bringing them up early for two reasons: First, to help you avoid choosing a title that may be inappropriate. Second, to alert you that there may not be any relationship between the title someone uses and the level of wisdom, knowledge, experience, or leadership ability that such a title would normally suggest.

Self-assumed titles are those you give to yourself; *earned titles* are bestowed upon you. The people behind the titles can be vastly different: I'll use a male example...

- At one extreme, imagine a 22-year-old man who's just discovered real-time BDSM. He assumes that because he's a man, he's a Dominant. More than that, he decides to introduce himself as, say, "Master Hugo" because he feels the *Master* title will give him *place* (stature, credibility) around the other men and women in the BDSM club.

- At the other extreme, you might meet a "Master Hugo" who's been involved with BDSM for decades, slowly gaining enough wisdom, skill, and seniority that other Masters, Dominants and submissives in the scene call him "Master Hugo."

In the first case, the title *Master* is hollow, based only on the man's ego and aspirations. He knows zip about zap. In the second case, the title *Master* is a recognition of actual rank and accomplishment, indicating that others consider this man to have mastered a body of knowledge and skills that make him capable of giving good advice or even judging others' capabilities. *This* Master Hugo could be a valuable resource for you, while the first could be almost anything— from a harmless poseur to a dangerous predator.

What makes this issue of titles even more confusing is that titles are often appropriate *within* a relationship. That is, if the Dom/me wants their sub to use *Master,* that's how it will be—it's just that the *Master* title does not automatically transfer outside the relationship. (Yes, some female Dominants want their property to refer to them as *Master* rather than *Mistress.* In this case, it's likely to be an issue of whether the Dominant—or D-type, as they are sometimes called—identifies as a Leatherwoman or as a FemDomme. No, I'm not going to explain that. You don't need to understand this right now.)

Addressing someone you don't know

How people within the BDSM community address others depends on a number of variables.

People usually refer to people exactly as they were first introduced to them. If you met someone as *Sir Stephen*, then for your purposes, that's his name even if you know that he's really Billy Johnson. As you gain seniority in this culture, people will start using *Sir/Ma'am* or even possibly *Master/Mistress* titles with you. These are public recognitions of your stature.

People may be casual about titles online or at a munch, but there is a higher level of etiquette (called *protocol*) required at a BDSM club meeting, play party, or any kind of fetish or Leather event where people are dressed up. When in doubt, follow the lead of those more experienced. If nobody is there to guide you, just remember that politeness is always appreciated. When in doubt about whether or not to use a title with someone, just ask how they wish to be addressed. A simple *Sir* or *Ma'am* is almost always acceptable.

It can be a little more challenging to figure out how to address a female dominant. *Mistress* is most commonly used in BDSM circles to refer to a female D-type (Domme, Owner, or Master), especially if the woman is a professional Dominatrix. However, some female dominants avoid using *Mistress* because historically this referred to the kept woman of a married man and they don't want any vanillas who hear that term to draw tawdry inferences.

Some women similarly avoid *Madam* because it used to describe the female owner of a brothel. (Note: I've recently learned that *Madam* is the preferred title given to a senior female Top in some BDSM communities.) You'll also find Dominant women who prefer to be called *Sir* or *Master* by their property: it depends upon the subculture they belong to.

Symbols

BDSM communities use symbols that reveal their identity to insiders but hide their identities from outsiders. This means that you can wear or display one or more of these symbols in public without drawing undue attention to yourself. Many symbols pass as a piece of jewelry or casual clothing.

While this is not the place to cover all the symbols used in our communities, it can be useful to know about those that are the most common, so I urge you to look them up online. For starters, the overall symbol for BDSM is called a *triskelion*. A triskelion is a circular figure comprising three curved branches radiating from a center and merging into the encompassing circle. To differentiate the BDSM symbol from the triskele used throughout history, there are three holes (or dots)—one in each of the three black fields— to represent the previously-described elements encompassed by the term BDSM: bondage and discipline (B&D), Dominance and submission (D/s), and sadomasochism (SM). Some people wear triskelion pins on their shirts, vests, or on charms around their necks. (Vests: you'll learn about *pin vests* as you gain experience in BDSM clubs.)

A collar, with or without a visible lock, is the most common symbol to signify that one is owned (whether as a slave, a pet, or other role). Anything worn around the neck can serve a couple as the symbolic collar: a leather dog collar, a rawhide bootlace, a steel chain, or a necklace that has a lock or key hanging from it. Collars can be relatively inconspicuous, especially if they can pass as jewelry or if they are worn beneath wearer's shirt. Collars can also be blaringly obvious BDSM symbols of ownership and, depending upon the social setting, can draw wanted/unwanted attention.

Other common ownership symbols include the slave bracelet (a ring connected to a matching bracelet by a thin chain) and the Ring of O, loosely based on the ring that the female slave character wears in the famous 20th-century BDSM novel *The Story of O* by Pauline Reage.

Along with wearable symbols, there are many specialty pride flag (also available as vest pins and patches) to signify your participation in one or another part of the overall BDSM culture. A few examples of flags or logos that identify BDSM subgroups include: Leather/BDSM, Master/slave, Pup or Pony play, slave Pride, Bootblacks, boy/boi Pride, and uniform fetishists, etc.

Symbolism can start out as a practical device but later become merely symbolic. For example, the handkerchief code—developed in the 1960s by kinky gay men—was originally a discreet way to signal one's sexual preferences and interests to others in the noisy and distracting environment of a "leather bar." A red, navy, black, or yellow hanky worn in the *left* rear pocket of denim or leather pants signaled, respectively, your interest in *giving* a fisting, cock-fucking, rough play, or piss play to someone else. Worn in the *right* rear pocket, the same colors signaled one's interest in *receiving* the same things as a bottom.

Over the years, however, the number of hanky colors and their supposed meanings grew to the point that the code is now mostly a joke. Various online lists include multiple subtle shades of each basic color as well as things like a checkerboard pattern, animal-paw prints, and miniature teddy bears to be worn right or left. No one can remember all of the variations, but it can be fun to read about them, and a selection of colored hankies in your appropriate pockets can make a good conversation starter—if anyone can see them!

BDSM vs. abuse

Before going any further into the customs, behaviors, and

complexities of this culture, I'd like to stop for a moment and confront head-on a topic that often arises when discussing BDSM. From the limited perspective of the general public (who believes that one person striking another for any reason is abuse), some rather routine BDSM activities (such as slapping, spanking, flogging, and so on) can be alarming if you're unused to the BDSM culture. In fact, such activities could be considered illegal in many states if witnessed by a law- enforcement office. But, and it's an important *but,* while BDSM activities may appear superficially similar to, say, assaults by an abusive spouse or domestic partner, they are vastly different in reality because the underlying *intention* is totally different.

Definition of abuse

The official distinctions between SM and abuse were carefully formulated by more than 20 organizations at the second Leather Leadership Conference, held in New York City in 1998. The conference concluded after creating a statement of *Principles and Guidelines* intended to help law enforcement and social services professionals understand the difference between abusive relationships and consensual SM.

I've reprinted some of the key conclusions/findings in this section of the book. The original wording is so clear that I've made no effort to edit it.

SM is a complex group of behaviors between consenting adults involving the consensual exchange of power and the giving and receiving of intense erotic sensation and/or mental discipline. SM includes intimate activities within the scope of informed consent that is freely given.

Abuse is: Physical, sexual or emotional acts inflicted on a person without their informed and freely given consent.

Principles: The SM-Leather-Fetish communities recognize the phrase "Safe, Sane, Consensual" as the best brief summary of principles guiding SM practices:

- **Safe** means knowing about the techniques and safety concerns involved in what you are doing and acting in accordance with that knowledge.
- **Sane** means knowing the difference between fantasy and reality and acting in accordance with that knowledge.
- **Consensual** means respecting the limits imposed by each participant at all times. *Safewords* represent one of the recognized ways to maintain limits to ensure that each participant can end his or her participation with a word or gesture. (NOTE: I'm going to spell "safeword" as one word; I know it's not usually written that way, but this is a *term* in the BDSM world.)

Guidelines: Informed consent must be judged by balancing the following criteria for each encounter at the time the acts occurred:

- Was informed consent expressly denied or withdrawn?
- Were there factors that negated the informed consent?
- What is the relationship of the participants?
- What was the nature of the activity?
- What was the intent of the accused abuser?

Tests for abuse in a relationship: Whether an individual's SM role is Top/Dominant or bottom/submissive, *abuse* may exist if you answer *no* to any of the following questions:

- Are your needs and limits respected?
- Is your relationship built on honesty, trust, and respect?
- Are you able to express feelings of guilt or jealousy or unhappiness?
- Can you function in everyday life?
- Can you refuse to do illegal activities?
- Can you insist on safe sex practices?
- Can you choose to interact freely with others outside of your relationship?

- Can you leave the situation without fearing that you will be harmed, or fearing the other participant(s) will harm themselves?

- Can you choose to exercise self-determination with money, employment, and life decisions?

- Do you feel free to discuss your practices and feelings with anyone you choose?

Some of the concepts referred to in this statement are discussed in more detail below, specifically *Safe, Sane, Consensual* or SSC (in a page or two), and *safewords* (in Chapter 4).

Kinds of abuse

First, let me be clear that an abuser's victim may well be their own partner whom they believe that they love. However, the perpetrator and the victim may have very different beliefs or attitudes about whether a particular set of behaviors are simply part of the submissive's training or outright abuse.

Abusers may use a number of ways to control their victim, none of which are acceptable in the context of a consensual, negotiated SM relationship. These actions cannot be stopped with a safeword, and can include:

- **Physical Abuse**: hitting, punching, choking, kicking, slapping, shoving, beating, leaving marks, or using weapons outside contract/scene limits and not respecting safewords. Defending these nonconsensual physical actions as the way *real* SM works.

- **Psychological abuse** (also referred to as emotional **abuse** or **mental abuse**): near-constant criticism, ridicule, false or misleading statements, criticizing their interest in something, humiliating or degrading them in public or private outside of contract/scene limits and not respecting safewords. Such abuse is often associated with situations of power imbalance, whether within a relationship, or in the workplace.

- **Sexual Abuse**: forcing sex, specific sex acts or sex with others; refusing to practice safer sex; refusing to negotiate or not respecting contract/scene limits; forcing SM acts during sex; or defending these nonconsensual physical actions as the way *real* SM works.

- **Economic Abuse**: controlling economic resources; stealing money, credit cards, or checks; running up debt; forcing you to live above your means; fostering total economic dependence; using economic status to determine relationship roles/norms, including purchase of food, clothes, etc.

- **Outing**: using awareness of fear and hatred of certain marginalized groups in our society. Threatening to out someone as being into SM, being gay, lesbian, bisexual, transgender, polyamorous, and/or being an illegal immigrant. Using society's prejudices as a way to control a person who is part of a marginalized group.

SSC—Safe, Sane, and Consensual

Some people have the false idea that SSC was originally formulated purely as a public-relations move— to make kinky erotic practices seem less threatening to the vanilla folks outside the scene, while those within the scene know better. That's just not so.

As used today, *playing by SSC standards* means that you're *playing with colors*. It means that if the sensations get too intense, the bottom can say *yellow* to slow down the action or say *red* to stop the action. Playing with colors means that the bottom has some control over the BDSM scene.

By playing by SSC standards, the Top is agreeing that the activities are not intended to cause *damage* or *harm* in the legal sense. Both parties are agreeing that the overall *intent* of their SM scene (play session) is to have fun: when the scene ends, both people should be talking about getting together to do it again.

You're following SSC guidelines if...

- the Top takes reasonable precautions to avoid causing harm that would affect the bottom's ability to go on with life
- the bottom is physically and psychologically prepared for the proposed activity *and* has disclosed to the Top any relevant medical or psychological disabilities, any use of drugs, and any personal limits (things they either cannot or will not do or accept).

Now, here is some amplification and clarification about the three elements of SSC—safe, sane, and consensual.

Safe: Safe does not mean without risk. A lot of people have read the word safe in the SSC formula in a naïve or literal way as meaning perfectly safe or risk-free. Some people have even tried to idiot-proof SM play by restricting what is allowed in BDSM clubs or events to play that can't possibly lead to any harm. Not surprisingly, this approach turns off the more adventurous members of our communities who either reject SSC outright or shift to RACK play standards (Risk Aware Consensual Kink— discussed in a few more pages.)

"Chanting 'safe, sane, and consensual' like a mantra can't save you from a bad scene or a bad relationship, and it can't replace the years of study and practice that guide an experienced Top or bottom, Dominant or submissive through the maze of choices both must confront. While 'safe, sane, and consensual' may suggest the outlines of an SM ethics, actually articulating one will take a lot more work than coining a useful slogan. But it's a start."

— *david stein*, who coined the phrase, from his essay on SSC (available at boybear.us)

Sane: *Sane* means that both players know what they are doing, have clear mental faculties, and are not angry, intoxicated, or in some other kind of altered mental state that may make them unable to distinguish fantasy from reality. It also means that the Top is playing ethically and within their level of training *and* has prepared the play area with appropriate safety equipment.

Consensual: Consensual means that both parties understand *and agree to* the proposed activities and *accept* the potential risks. A scene is *not* consensual if:

- You did *not* expressly agree to it beforehand. That doesn't mean you have to sign a contract or utter any specific words as long as your *intention* is clear.

Origins of SSC

Some people have the false idea that SSC was originally formulated purely as a public-relations move—to make kinky erotic practices seem less threatening to the vanilla folks outside the scene, while those within the scene know better. That's just not so.

Safe, Sane, and Consensual was a slogan used by the Leather/SM Contingent in the 1987 March on Washington for Lesbian and Gay Rights. It is a concept that subsequently spread widely in both homosexual and heterosexual BDSM circles.

(Just nodding your head at the right time or saying "Yes" when asked if you agree can be enough to give consent.)

- You agreed to some aspect of the proposed play because you were afraid to say "No." That's coercion, not consent, and it means, at the very least, that you probably shouldn't be involved with that Top.

- You expressly withdraw your consent during the scene, but the Top continued the play (this is called *playing through red*).

- You *want* to withdraw your consent during the scene, but you're gagged or otherwise unable to communicate, and the Top makes no attempt to check in with you to confirm that you're still okay with what's happening.

There are many other subtle issues involved in consenting to BDSM activity, and I'll revisit this topic several times in the   course of the book. It's important to be as clear as possible about consent because this distinguishes SM or BDSM from abuse.

SSC play standards

Because some of the things we do in BDSM are dangerous, and because even the lightest activities can carry real risks, our communities have developed some rules for play.

When an accident happens, it is either a true accident or the Top is at fault. Either the Top was insufficiently trained or was playing beyond their skill level. A person who makes this kind of mess usually becomes known and, depending upon the severity, is often shunned thereafter in the community. (NOTE: In some rare cases, accidents occur because the bottom did not fully communicate their limits or concerns.)

Here are some of the other subtleties of SSC play:

- **Limits**: *Before play starts* (during scene negotiation), the bottom gets to accept or exclude the proposed SM activities. For example, you might say, "paddling and spanking are fine, but no flogging or whipping; light bondage only; must use condoms for intercourse; no urine or scat; heavy tit play but no piercing or electricity." Talking this to death can kill the erotic energy, but the Top will be flying blind unless both parties agree upon what they want to do and have done to them. (Note: please see the section titled, "A word about Saying Yes and No" in Chapter 5 for a very important expansion about determining limits.)

- **Safewords:** *During play*, safewords are a recognized way to maintain limits. Those of us who believe in the KISS system (Keep It Simple, Stupid) just use the colors *red, yellow,* and *green*. This red/yellow/green method is called the stoplight system. For instance, if the bottom says *yellow*, the Top knows that *something is* going on that needs to be checked out. This is **not** a request to *stop* the play—but the Top needs to determine whether

A core truth

A bottom has the right to expect that the Top knows the safety and danger issues associated with the proposed SM activities and knows how to reduce or control risk of accident. That's the core rule. But it should never be assumed.

the bottom is asking only to slow it down a bit so they can process the sensations or perhaps not to do some particular technique because it hurts and is affecting their enjoyment of the scene. Clearly, if *red* is the agreed-upon safeword and the bottom says *red* during a scene, the Top is ethically bound to stop the action altogether.

Saying *red* (or whatever word has been chosen to mean *stop*) indicates that the bottom has withdrawn consent for the Top to continue: the bottom must be released immediately (and be cared for). Any uncommonly used word can become a safeword, but (as I just said) simplicity is your friend and *red* is the default safeword in most public play parties.

There is a refinement to calling *yellow*. Rather than saying *yellow*, the bottom may call out a body part that needs the Top's attention. When the bottom says the word foot, for example, the Top will

"Just because you consent to play does not mean that you consent to everything. You have the right to set limits.

— *Sabrina Santiago,* nelaonline.org

Some messages for tops

Your word is your bond: You are judged in this community by your word. Your actions are the physical manifestation of your word.

Your ability to remain in good standing in this community hinges on your ethics and your responsible action. You want play partners? Play ethically and honorably.

The submissives' network spreads news about as rapidly as drum beats in the Amazonian jungles. Before you wake up the next morning, lots of people will know what you've done— or not done.

While the Top's job is often to push a bottom to the edge of (and slightly beyond) their comfort zone, you have serious responsibilities in this regard:

• To know your skill level and not play beyond it,
• To know how to read your bottom and not play beyond a clear or implied call to stop.

stop immediately to address the bottom's foot. The binding may be tight and with a quick adjustment the problem is relieved and the play can continue. Saying a body part as a *yellow* gets the message to the Top that this is not a slow-down or pre- red request by the bottom—it's just a *pay attention to this specific thing* notification before the scene continues.

•**Why use safewords?** After all, what's wrong with saying, "Wait, please, I need to process that last cane strike" when you need a break or "Ouch! Stop that right now, George— I'm done!" when you've had enough? *Nothing* is wrong with that, and it's one reason many experienced, ethical players prefer to do without safewords. Safewords are especially useful in role-playing scenes— like a simulated rape or kidnapping—where the bottom wants to be able to say things like, "No! Stop, George! Don't!" *without meaning them.* If it's important for the bottom to protest, struggle, and try to get away while really wanting the action to continue, then substituting the safeword *red* for "Stop, George, and I mean it!" is just the ticket.

- **Safewords aren't magical**: Other than to let senior members of the community know about the incident after the fact, there may not be much a bottom can do at the time if the Top *fails* to stop on *red*. Safewords assume that you're playing with an ethical and responsible Top who respects limits and honors promises; unfortunately, that's not always the case. The safeword system can also break down if you're gagged (though there are some workarounds) or *flying* on adrenaline and endorphins. In the latter cases, you'll lack the presence of mind to evaluate your condition rationally

We also use SSC *within* our communities for a number of specific reasons:

- It's a community guideline or standard that most of us agree on at least roughly.
- It encourages all kinky players to think about the safety requirements of their favorite activities and take appropriate precautions.
- It declares to the world that we are normal and not psychologically damaged in some way.
- It helps ensure that we are playing with willing people who understand the risks
- It's a safety net for newcomers.

Let me expand on that last point.

Following the SSC/safeword model can protect both of you if you are playing with someone fairly new to BDSM (or new to YOU). In theory, Tops who haven't yet learned their bottom's preferences, limits, and body language can then rely on them simply *saying* when

A cautionary note

A Top who violates SSC rules in public play can do nearly irreparable damage to their reputation. In one recent dramatic case, a well-known and highly experienced professional Domme was banished from a cluster of clubs in a major West Coast city for irresponsible behavior that sent her play partner to the ER with injuries that ultimately required facial-reconstruction surgery.

to slow down or stop. In reality, though, many new bottoms aren't sure when to speak up and when to just go along with the new experience. Experienced players sometimes compare safe- words to training wheels on a bicycle: If you need them to get started, it's wise to put your pride away and use them. Bottoms are as responsible as Tops for scenes turning out well.

CAUTIONARY NOTE: Safewords only work when bottoms use them *and* Tops respect them. A predatory Top can make SSC noises in negotiation and then ignore safewords during a scene. Get to know the *person* you're playing with before you play. At their core, both vanilla and BDSM relationships revolve around trust and trustworthiness.

RACK—Risk Aware Consensual Kink

Bottom line: When someone says that they play by RACK standards, it means that they are playing without colors. There is no *red*.

Well… "*There is no red*" is not precisely true. First, those senior enough to be using RACK standards are also senior enough to know how to read their bottoms; they know when they're pushing their bottom's boundaries and they are still responsible for playing with integrity.

Second, there are some advanced situations where the Top sets out with intention to push the bottom through some experience.

Again, so long as this is being done with honor and integrity, respecting the psychological and physical impact on the bottom, the BDSM community goes along with it. Third, at this level of play, the Top and bottom are almost always in a committed relationship; it's unlikely that the Top is going to do any hot-dogging in a scene that threatens the relationship to which they are both going home in a few hours (that's not in the Top's best interest). So while RACK doesn't play with colors, it still plays with honor and integrity

Now for some background-and-fill.

RACK evolved because some senior BDSM players pointed out that SSC rules create a psychological conflict for those involved in Power Exchange relationships. The argument is that if the Dom/me is *really in* charge of the person as well as the scene (as SSC rules dictate), then using *red* and *yellow* by their own s-types violates the most basic rules of these relationships. After all, a slave/property does not have the personal authority to say what can or cannot be done to them whether in or out of an SM scene. Again, I'm not going to be explaining *BDSM relationships* in this book (please see: *BDSM Mastery—Relationships: a guide for creating mindful relationships for Dominants and submissives* by Robert J. Rubel, Ph.D. and M. Jen Fairfield (Book Two in the BDSM Mastery Series).

SSC play guidelines gives way to RACK guidelines under either of two general conditions:

- Both parties are used to playing together. RACK play is appropriate when the Top knows their skill level and can be trusted to play within it, knows the bottom's limits and how to read their nonverbal signals, and knows how to adjust the intensity of sensations to match the bottom's ability to process the experience.
- An experienced couple is living in a Dominant/submissive, Master/slave, or Owner/property relationship. RACK play is common here because the rules of the relationship recognize that the person serving as Top makes relationship-appropriate decisions about the kind and intensity of play with their partner.

There are two principal objections to RACK. One objection is that in correcting SSC's tendency to downplay risks, RACK over-emphasizes them, leading people to think that advanced BDSM players are scary. Another objection with RACK is with the word *aware*. Some argue that it does no good to be *aware* of risks unless you actively work to minimize them. RACK explicitly recognizes that SM play can be dangerous— that's why it's reserved for advanced players. As a point of interest, Tops playing at this level are usually more focused on *connecting with their partners and riding the ride* than on *skill proficiency*.

Following RACK rather than SSC standards doesn't mean that senior Dom/mes, Masters, and Owners don't play safely or sanely, but it does mean that *they* are the people deciding what is safe and sane for their own property. *Consent* is considered implicit in these relationships. That their property is willing to remain with them and serve as their bottom constitutes ongoing consent.

There can sometimes appear to be a fine line between abuse and not-abuse. Ultimately, the needle points one way or the other based on the Top's intentions.

RACK and SSC realities

Okay, you have now read through the obligatory material on SSC and RACK that will enable you to be politically correct when speaking with other BDSMers. Now for a dose of reality from those that have been doing this a while.

Joseph Bean, one of the major thinkers and writers about BDSM and Leather, wrote a very interesting article titled: "The SSC Mistake" that appears on www.withinreality.com. In that article, he points out that by imposing standards on BDSM, others come to judge YOUR play based on THEIR understanding of what *safe, sane, and consensual* or *risk aware consensual kink* looks like (or feels like) in real time.

david stein, the person who came up with the SSC slogan in the firs place (and a gentleman of equal stature to Joseph Bean) comments in "How to Do the Right Kinky Thing: ethical principles for BDSM" that neither SSC nor RACK are, in fact, principles: SSC and RACK are slogans that, "at best remind us of some issues we need to think about in order to make good choices in BDSM. At worst, they promote complacency without providing any useful guidance." He goes on to say that there are no guarantees in life and you're not necessarily *safe* when you *sanely* cross a street, and being *aware* that crossing streets can be risky is secondary to your decision to *trust* that the approaching cars won't hit you. Which brings him to the key point: in BDSM, *consent* is not nearly as important as establishing and demonstrating that you are a *trustworthy* person. Trust, honor, and integrity will bring you many play partners

Reasons to be discreet

While I suspect that most of this is intuitive for you, I'd like to take a few pages to discuss discretion and our kinky world.

Being publicly kinky in a big city is different than being publicly kinky in a rural area; being out in the Bible Belt is different from being out on the West Coast or in New England. This section describes some areas to consider as you're considering sharing your interest or involvement in BDSM.

Employment: The way you dress or groom yourself, the symbols you choose to display, and the topics you chat about at work or online can all cause you to fail a job interview, to miss a promotion, or to lose your job altogether. And beyond whatever clues about your kinky life you leave yourself, it's sadly common for someone to be outed at work (or to their family) by someone else, whether purposely or accidentally. That's the current reality in the U.S.

Here are some true situations for the ladies to consider:

- You're freshly collared (this is like being engaged) and very, very proud and excited about it. So, do you wear your collar to work? (Does it look like a necklace or is it clearly a BDSM collar?)

- What if your Master orders you to wear it to work? Does their authority extend to your job? Will they (can they) support you if you obey and *lose* your job?

- Your Master wishes you always to refer to them as *Master*. They call you at work, and your office-mate overhears you saying, "Yes, Master, I'll take care of that, Master." You hang up to find your office-mate stunned; can you explain yourself?

- Suppose you wear a slave bracelet to work and someone asks about it, perhaps even naming it correctly. What do you say?

Moral: A little preplanning goes a long way.

Family and Friends: Being *out* to your friends puts many aspects of your future in their hands; you now must rely heavily upon *their* honor, ethics, and integrity to keep your secrets. Not all friends are *friends*, and not all of your friends today will be your friends tomorrow, if you get my drift. You'll need to decide how much you can trust each one. As a result, most heterosexuals who practice BDSM today use invented scene names and keep their real lives as private as they can.

The thing of it is, as you become increasingly involved in this way of life, the more you'll want to tell your friends and loved ones about your remarkable experiences. The more you realize that BDSM is a whole lot of fun, the more you'll want to share your enthusiasm. While some may understand and tolerate your general interest in BDSM, you'll probably not be invited to describe the details.

Children at home: With underage children living at home, you have one clear path: lock **everything** up and try to prevent your kids from discovering your nontraditional sex life. You don't want a visit from your local Child Protective Services; they're not going to be BDSM friendly. If your child can describe your BDSM gear, activities, or protocols, you're at risk of losing custody of *all* your children. When children are involved, no one in government—not the police, not the social-welfare bureaucracy, not elected officials and not the courts—will be sympathetic to your personal sexual needs or preferences. Examples abound.

Accidents happen, so be prepared when your child finds some piece of BDSM equipment you left out and asks what it is and why it's in the house. Similarly, you'll want to have an answer prepared for when your teenager stumbles across BDSM references, or even actual sites, online and asks you about them. You might wish to spend some time working up an explanation if they stumble across some BDSM link that *you* left up on your computer.

It is difficult to hide every hint of a BDSM lifestyle; if nothing else, nuances in your relationship dynamics with your partner can leap out to others as **different**. I'm just urging you to be prepared. For example, how are you going to handle a chance meeting out in public: "Mommy, why did that man call you *Linda*?"

A suggestion: With forethought and planning, you can teach your children that the two of you respect, trust, and love one another and consider each other's needs when making plans or reaching decisions that affect the family. You can also teach them about boundaries and how there are consequences for behavior that disrespects boundaries. You can teach them about power differentials in relationships and how these can be handled responsibly. Without anyone else noticing, you can make the good things about D/s or M/s parts of their lives. If you can hide the bedroom or playroom activities reasonably well and can teach your children the values that attracted you to one another in the first place, I believe you'll succeed in bringing up responsible, loving, and tolerant adults.

Since ethical BDSM is *not* abusive or degrading, living it with integrity won't hurt your children unless you disregard their needs by playing in front of them. Of course, you can get in a lot of trouble with the authorities even for purely vanilla sexual behavior in front of your children, so BDSM is not uniquely problematic in this respect.

Chapter 2
Big Touchy Topics

BDSM and sex—an allegory

Sex means different things to different people. What *sex* means to you changes as you learn more about your sexual options. Because BDSM is so rich and diversified, because it can cover so many elements and accommodate so many personal preferences and idiosyncrasies, your first exposure to the sexual side of BDSM can be a little intimidating. Actually, it can be a *lot* intimidating. To illustrate my point, I'm going to make up a little story about a mountain and mountain climbers.

For this exercise, please imagine that you've gone with your partner on a mountain vacation to do a little hiking—possibly some rock climbing, as a recent movie about it has made you both interested. You arrive at the park by late morning and spend some time admiring the beautiful view—the flowers, the lake, and the mountains. One mountain has caught your eye, and you and your partner start discussing ways of exploring it. As you stand there, you notice a stream of people locking up their cars, putting on backpacks and heading directly up the trail for the mountain. But you're not really in a hurry; it's a lovely day, so you decide to pitch a tent, set up two folding chairs, pour a couple of nice drinks and enjoy the romantic setting. After all, it's comfortable in the park and it looks like a lot of work to climb the mountain. Anyway, there are lots of other people camped down here.

Now let's talk sex. Let's think of that mountain as a big mountain of sexual exploration—and you're down in the campground. For this little story, being *down in the campground* means that your sex is playful but fairly routine, perhaps on a really good night or on a really hot date, the sex can get just a bit edgy and include love bites and love taps. But your sexual play is certainly not up to porn-movie standards. So—for the sake of our story—as you're looking at the other campers around you, you're seeing a sea of sexual activity. And their sex is vanilla—fucking, sucking, fingering—with only a few mildly interesting positions.

You scan the campground and then the mountainside with your powerful binoculars. Suddenly you realize that the sex play in the campground is not quite as inventive as the sex play that you can see a little higher up. As you focus the lenses, you find couples who are using silk blindfolds and some naughty spanking; this is defiantly more inventive than what is going on in the campground— or anything *you've* ever done. (Oh: how can you see them in that detail? They're exhibitionists, for starters. Anyway, the binoculars are magical. Stop being so literal!)

So, as you scan the mountain looking for others, you nudge your partner and point; there actually *is* more going on up there—quite a bit more. And, it looks *very interesting.* A little titillated, the two of you decide that you'll start climbing that mountain first thing in the morning.

The morning comes and off you go. You get to the level that you'd seen from the campground and your sex play becomes a little more interesting. After a while, though, you stop playing and look around with your binoculars and see that still further up, others seem to be having a raucous time—that's when the word *edgy* enters your mind.

The steepness changes as you climb; as you are about to step off the grassy slopes onto exposed rock, a couple near you explains that you have to rope up for safety reasons. "Rope up?" you ask— the phrase making no sense to you at the moment.

They lend you some Goldline, show you how to tie in, and lead you higher. After a while, you see that there are rock outcroppings that you know (from the movies) will require a certain amount of technical skill to surmount. Some folks climbing alongside you see that you're unsure about what to do and stop to help you. They show you how to select the correct piton for various situations, they teach you how to know that the piton is set correctly, and they show you how to tie in to a belay position. They even show you how to rappel with and without a harness.

You are well past the stage of silk scarves and playful spankings; you are well past the stage of rabbit vibrators and traditional porn; you're actively exploring BDSM. With some amusement, you and your partner realize that your sexual play now looks pretty sharp and pointy to those gazing up at you from below. Trying to be helpful, you call down to them to take climbing courses, to read books and to practice. You tell them that this is the climb of a lifetime. Every so often, one or two of the watchers starts to climb. Most of them think you're nuts.

After your new climbing buddies assure you that you're good to go, the two of you set off again. As you gain altitude, you notice that fewer and fewer people are climbing beside you. This does not bother those in your climbing group, of course, as it is all a matter of taste.

But you, too, continue to look up and you see that there are actually more people above you than you'd thought. You now realize that *the more you learned, the more you learned to see*. Your mountaineering skills have now increased to the point that you are loaded down with tens of pounds of mountaineering tools like rope, pitons, carabineers, and even a Jumar Ascender. You are ready to start climbing the sheer rock face. You grab on to fire play; you side-step carotid play; you rest for a minute on mindfuck. You're cutting new personal ground and you've never known anyone who had a climb quite like this one.

Many who enjoy BDSM like things to be as intense as possible. Maybe you're one of them and maybe you're not, but chances are, no matter who you are, you fall somewhere on a line that includes things like tying your partner up or being tied up yourself, giving or getting a light (or heavy) spanking, biting gently or hard, or even hitting your partner in the stomach at the moment of climax.

Taking charge during sex is fun because it gives you an opportunity to play with your role as a lover. For a moment, you're not so tender— instead, you're cruel, mean, and intense. But, in order to cross the lines, you must first define them.

It's up to both of you.

It's what this book is about.

Red flag

Girls don't like *creepers;* girls don't like guys who act weird. Red flags are behavioral warning signs that something is not quite right. These behaviors are not specific to any gender, sexual orientation, or relationship structure. While these warning flags apply equally to straight folk and kinky folk, you probably have a statistically greater chance of finding some disturbed folk in our BDSM world simply because of what it is that we do to amuse ourselves. Predators can hide more easily here.

Now, someone with one, two, or five of the behaviors in the list you're about to read may raise your eyebrows, but when you find groups of repeating, negative behaviors from this list, you'll want to be on alert. The more of these behaviors someone exhibits, the stronger the chance that something is psychologically wrong with them. Since "something wrong with them" can mean a lot of trouble for you, this is an important section of this book.

My strong message to you is this: Take your time in establishing new relationships, for it may take time for these behaviors or patterns to emerge. When you see these behaviors, I'd suggest that you slow down or even stop the relationship in order to assess your situation. Generally, the more of these behaviors you observe in a person (and the more often you see them and the quicker they emerge in a new relationship), the more you are at risk for being emotionally and/or physically harmed by this person.

Categorized list of potentially alarming behaviors

As I was researching red flag behaviors I ran across an exceptional blog by a woman named Epiphany. She said that Saikiji Kitalpha from *Second Life* was the author and that, in the original posting, Saikiji had said that anyone could reproduce it, but please give her the credit. Saikiji, you did a great job! (What follows is only slightly edited.)

Before you start reading these lists, please recognize that while you may find some of these behaviors in most people, you won't fin clusters of them in people who are psychologically and emotionally safe and stable. If you find yourself saying, "Gosh, these really fit X," then you may wish to take a step even farther back from X and ask yourself if this is really a person who fits we l into your own life.

A caution: Not all of us are born with neuro-typical brain wiring. A substantial (and apparently growing) number of us (myself included) fall somewhere on the Autism spectrum and exhibit certain unusual social behaviors. You might wish to familiarize yourself with Autism Spectrum Disorder traits, as many of us exhibit social oddness that can be off-putting at best and alarming at worst. But that's different than being dangerous for you, and that's what this section is about.

Tries to isolate you:

- Tries to limit your access to others in your life: friends, family, and BDSM community.
- Forbids contact with others or undermines relationships or activities.
- Is negative and unsupportive of your other (established) relationships.
- Monitors your communications (e-mails, phone calls, chats).
- May want you to quit your job or give up your car or telephone or control your finances
- Monitors your activities, demands to know where you've been and whom you've been with—often in an accusatory manner.
- Habitually calls and/or visits unexpectedly.
- Refuses to allow you a safe-call (discussed in depth in Chapter 4).
- Becomes angry if you question them or show signs of independence or strength.

Is deceptive:

- Is reluctant to give you personal and factual information about themselves.
- Refuses to give their marital status when asked before a firs meeting.
- Gives inconsistent or conflicting information or details about themselves or past events.
- Has very limited times/places/methods where you are able to contact them and gets angry if you try to make contact outside of those conditions.
- Does not give you their home or work phone numbers at the appropriate time.
- Has multiple online identities for interacting within the same communities.

- Cheats on you.
- Gives the impression of being very successful without any evidence of real success.
- Disappears from communication for days or weeks at a time without explanation.
- Is evasive about their activities, especially unexplained absences.
- Primarily interacts with you in a kinky or sexual manner, as if role-playing.
- Will not have normal, everyday vanilla conversations.

Behaves oddly:

- Your friends warn you against the person.
- Is critical of the public BDSM community and will not participate in BDSM clubs/munches/parties.
- Is critical of many respected members of the BDSM community and has interpersonal conflicts with other BDSMers.
- Has no apparent BDSM references or friends you can talk to and becomes angry, changes the topic, answers questions with questions, or ends the conversation when you ask personal questions or ask for references.
- May give you (made up) names of "friends," but you can't verify that they even exist.
- Has bad or no relationship with their biological family.

Seems insecure:

- Often exaggerates.
- Deflects blame to others for things going wrong and resorts to extreme measures to prove that they, themselves, are not at fault.
- Does not take personal responsibility when things go badly; they will not acknowledge their own mistakes.

- Their apologies feel insincere, phony, or are insulting.
- Puts you down in front of others.
- Is constantly comparing themselves to others.
- Brags excessively about their experience, scene credentials, mastery, or training.
- Engages in scene name-dropping.
- Avoids discussing what your possible future relationship could be like. Tries to keep you in the dark about what might happen next in the relationship.
- Seems not to reveal their emotional side, hides their vulnerabilities or behaves in an emotionless manner.
- Hides behind their D/s authority, demands that their authority not be questioned.

Is disrespectful:

- Does not respect your feelings, rights, or opinions.
- Is rude to public servers such as waitresses, cashiers, and janitors.
- Displays little concern or awareness of the feelings or needs of others.
- Never or seldom says "thank you," "excuse me," or "I am sorry" to anyone.
- Exhibits obvious and excessive displays of impatience.
- Believe that they deserve some particular reward or benefit even at the expense of others.

Is manipulative:

- Tries to make you feel guilty for not being *good enough*.
- Says that you are not a *true* sub/slave/Dom.
- Belittles your ideas.
- Blames you for their own hurt feelings and anger outbursts.
- Blames you for all relationship problems.

- Yells or threatens to withdraw their love or leave you if you do not do as they wish.

Is inconsistent:

- Does not keep their word; breaks promises.
- Makes plans with you, then makes excuses for changing those plans.
- Treats you lovingly and respectfully one day and then harshly and accusingly the next.
- Goes through extreme highs (behaving with great kindness) and pronounced lows (behaving with cruelty), almost as though they are two distinctly different people.

Is domineering:

- Pressures you into doing things you do not want to do.
- Does not respect your limits, negotiations, or contracts.
- Pushes you too quickly into a D/s or M/s or polyamorous relationship.
- Pushes you into a sexual relationship too fast.
- Overly demanding of your time; must be the center of your attention.
- Insists safewords or safe-calls are not necessary.

Is intemperate:

- Conspicuous consumption: spends money largely and inappropriately on luxury items.
- Abuses alcohol or other drugs.
- Gambles excessively.
- Constantly asks for money or material goods from you or others.
- Falls in love with you way too fast; swears undying love before even meeting you.

- Begins saying things like, "I can't live without you," or "Do what you want with me," or "I don't have any limits."
- Deliberately says or does things that result in getting themselves hurt.

Is temperamental:

- Loses control of their emotions in arguments. Raises their voice, yells, calls you names, blames you for things they did.
- Uses force or violence to solve problems.
- Punches walls or throws things when upset.
- Turns on their peers, going quickly from *best friend* to *arch enemy*, often for trivial or imagined reasons.
- Speaks badly of others, particularly of people with whom they once were good friends.
- Displays a disproportionately negative reaction to being told *no*.
- Holds excessive grudges against others and goes to great lengths to get revenge on people.
- Threatens suicide or other forms of self-harm.
- Hypersensitive and easily upset by annoyances that are part of daily life.

Has certain established behaviors:

- They, themselves, were victims of abuse. (Their abuse may be a learned behavior.)
- May exhibit cruel behavior towards animals.
- Might admit to hitting a partner in the past, but claims the partner made them do it.

Quite a list, but please remember that many of these traits are normal or standard behavior for people; it is the cluster of several of these that build into red flags.

This point brings us neatly to the next section.

Don't get involved with someone who wants to *break* you

Occasionally, someone asks me how to psychologically break down a submissive in order to build the person back up in ways they wish.

Every so often—particularly on the less-sophisticated Internet hookup sites—you'll find ads for people seeking to be "broken." I strongly suspect that most of these people are living in the Internet world of fantasy-BDSM, but who knows? Perhaps they've just seen movies (such as *The Pet*) and/or read fiction about using physical force and terror to strip a person's ego-defenses in order to retrain them to behave and react exactly as the trainer wishes them to.

Couple of things. First, psychological brainwashing is, by definition, non-consensual. Second, even if they were a licensed and credentialed psychologist or psychiatrist, it is unethical to *break* someone like that. Those professions are for healing, not molding someone to their own will.

Please be clear: the way I'm using the word *breaking* in a BDSM training context is different than *behavior modification* as psychologists mean it. As few people know much about psychology, many new Tops and bottoms ask these kinds of *breaking* questions because it's part of the stereotype that BDSM is about breaking someone's spirit/will, presumably based on the other stereotype that BDSM is about pain and punishment.

Someone who is considering engaging in an unsafe non-consensual activity with another person either…

- realizes the risks and is willing to proceed anyway (suggesting sadistic behavior that may turn out to include criminal intent), or
- does not understand or appreciate what they are contemplating, and thus has an *altered sense of reality*—a

classic definition of insanity.

NOTE: It may be hard to tell that someone has an altered sense of reality, particularly if they are well-versed in the jargon of our culture. Again—*caution* is the byword.

Important rules for playing

As you'll realize by the time you've finished this book, there aren't a great many truly fundamental *rules* about BDSM play. However, the rules and customs that have evolved over the years are particularly important, and you would disregard them at your own peril.

Listen to your gut

If you get a sixth sense feeling that something isn't going exactly right (or at least not the way you'd thought it would go) during initial negotiations or during a scene, say something. You remain responsible for yourself even when you're tied to a Saint Andrew's Cross or spanking bench. Some who are new to our culture think that once they enter negotiations, they have to end up playing because they began by asking for the activity. This just isn't so.

Within our community there is a shared responsibility to watch out for others. If you're watching a play scene and notice that something doesn't seem quite right, please say something to the Dungeon Monitor (Dungeon Monitor or DM: an experienced safety monitor) or to a senior BDSM person. Chances are that everything is okay, but accidents can happen—particularly when a Top goes into Top- space. Once in Topspace—and focused on the bottom's reactions— it's possible to miss reactions of those watching. We'll be discussing Topspace and subspace a bit later.

Much harm can come from thinking, "Well, that just doesn't seem right, but I guess that is the way it is done. After all, he's the Dom." Trust yourself, no matter how new you may be. If your Dom/me or Master wants you to do something that violates your personal code of ethics, you must explain your position. If your partner ridicules you for taking that stand or ignores your view about the topic, you have valuable information to help you decide whether to keep them in your life.

Only play sober

Conventional wisdom advises people not to drink or use recreational drugs before or during SM play. Conventional wisdom is correct. First, you can't provide "informed consent" when you're drunk or high, and few Tops or bottoms will play with anyone in that state. Second, SM activities can be dangerous. Prudence (and the concern you have for your partner) demands that your judgment and reaction times are unimpaired during play.

Specifically, in order to know when to add, stabilize, change, or reduce the sensations being administered, the Top must remain accurate with regard to skill-based play **and also** remain fully alert to the bottom's subtle and not- so-subtle body signals. The bottom that has taken mind- altering substances may not be fully aware of what the Top is doing to their body—and thus is not giving off the same body- signals that they would if they were sober. I need hardly point out that this is a risky condition to be in when the activity is as potentially dangerous as ours.

While some SM activities (such as spanking or erotic flogging) are *not* normally very dangerous, others (such as caning, knife play, fire play, etc.) can be *very* dangerous, indeed.

The reasons for avoiding drugs and alcohol before and during play are slightly different for the Top and bottom.

For the Top:

- Drugs can impair depth perception and also cause you to lose track of your personal strength. This can affect many activities, such as caning, flogging, and whipping. A misapplied cane stroke or whip-strike can end a scene in a heartbeat.

If you get a sixth sense feeling that something is wrong about a person, act on that feeling. If the guy's a little creepy or if the girl appears to be a high-maintenance drama queen, ask people about it. Even if everyone to whom you speak supports this person, if your uneasy feeling persists, I urge you to conclude that this is not the right person for you and move on.

Not everyone is for everyone and some people are for no one.

- On drugs, altered reaction time can affect most aspects of play, particularly if you're surprised by some aspect of the play and need to react quickly, such as in fire play, suspension play, and knife play.

- Mind-altering substances usually affect observation skills, making it more difficult not only to read the bottom's signals but also make it more difficult to react to those signals with appropriate caution and concern.

- Impaired judgment can also lead a Top to do crazy stuff and/ or play beyond their skill level. Tops that have had a little something before play are more likely than those that are stone-cold sober to want to try something unusual. *Unusual* seldom ends well.

For the bottom:

- The most obvious point is that to the extent that your mind is dulled, you will miss the very experiences that you had hoped to gain from bottoming with this Top.

- The second most obvious point is that mind-altering substances will dull your critical mind. When under some influence, you are likely to permit the Top to do things to you that you would not permit if you were sober. You're likely to let a Top try something new on you when you are in that "Sure, why not?" frame of mind. This is not a good idea. Not with SM play.

- Perhaps most seriously, you may find it more difficult even to know whether you are being hurt. You may not be sure when to call *yellow* or *red*. You can get hurt. You will be surprised that you're hurt. In the extreme, you may lose the ability to know when to stop the scene. (I've had this happen to a friend of mine.)

Play within your skill level

The trouble is, you don't know what you don't know: this is referred to as unconscious incompetence. When you start out doing SM play, you can be dangerous.

In daily life, if you try to do something you don't know how to do, the worst outcome is that you've put something together wrong, said something that showed your ignorance, hurt someone's feeling, and/or made some incorrect assumptions. Maybe you're a little over confident or maybe you're a bit of an ass (welcome to the club). The thing of it is, in SM play, there can be real consequences for doing something you really don't know how to do.

In our world, the consequences of engaging in SM play when in a mentally altered state and/ or when you have been poorly trained can be horrific. Just to make sure we're on the same page, I'll relate a true story that can be the poster-child that defines **horrific**. This is a true story.

The fire play scene was set up in either a public dungeon or a private play party (I don't remember); however the first- person account of this incident mentioned that there was no DM. The bottom was handcuffed to a stainless steel medical table that was designed to contain body fluids (that is, liquids will remain pooled on the table rather than flowing onto the floor). The Top had been drinking at the play party, although it's unknown how much liquor he had consumed.

This was to have been an alcohol-wanding fire play scene; the Top's training was unknown. Rather than soak the fire wand in alcohol and apply a controllable swath of the stuff that could then be lit and quickly put out, the Top poured some amount of alcohol

Drugs and alcohol are prohibited at many (but certainly not all) BDSM parties. If someone is observed violating those rules others may take it as a sign that this person (these people) are not fully in charge of themselves. The reasoning is simple: they knew that drugs and alcohol were prohibited and chose to use them anyway. That represents a character flaw. Depending upon the severity of the specific episode, this can lead to being banned from future parties and possibly even from a club.

(NOTE: Inappropriate behavior at a club event or play party tends to arise among people who are a bit new to BDSM and who don't yet understand the BDSM cultural rules. New Dom/mess adopt the attitude that they have a right to do whatever they wish since they are a Dominant. They see the world of BDSM as a world ruled by Dominants, and since they are one (a dominant), they must be a ruler. But, it just ain't so, to paraphrase the great baseball player Yogi Berra. It may take years for some people to pass out of the asshole stage—some never do.)

directly onto the bound bottom's tummy. Some unknown amount of the fluid flowed under her body

When the Top ignited the alcohol on her tummy—the target area of the scene—much of the table erupted in flame. Bound to the table, she could not escape. While there might or might not have been a fire extinguisher in the room, the victim who wrote about this episode did not mention anyone trying to put her out with a fire extinguisher. The Top did not follow standard fire play safety practices: he did not have a "second" backing him up and holding a fire extinguisher.

The bottom was burned extensively and was hospitalized for some time. (She has long-since posted this story and photos on FetLife and has given me permission to retell the story. I use it when teaching fire play—one of my specialties.)

As they relate to this story, here are the safety violations relevant to what is called *alcohol wanding*, a form of fire play:

- Rule One: Never bind the bottom in any way when conducting any kind of **open flame** play (flash cotton, alcohol wanding, fire flogging, wax play)

- Rule Two: In public play, always have a trained DM or senior club member serve as your backup. That person's job is to stand near the Top (but out of the Top's way) and hold a fire extinguisher with the safety pin already removed. In case of an emergency, the Top is responsible for attending to the bottom; the backup person is responsible for putting out the fire. (In private play, the fire extinguisher must be within the Top's easy reach, safety pin removed.)

- Rule Three: The stabilized bottle holding the alcohol must not be on the same table/surface as the bottom and should be lidded/capped/covered.

Some forms of SM play require competent training before you can try them on someone. Most BDSM clubs offer education programs, and how-to books and DVDs are readily available. Learn what you can on your own, then get checked out by a qualified senior Dom/me known for that skill. We're a helpful lot and none of us want you to hurt someone.

A suggestion for bottoms: If you are about to play with a new Top and that person has not sat down with you to discuss such things as limits, health issues, and safewords, I recommend you reconsider what you are about to do. *You are responsible for being responsible.* You are giving your body to someone to play with: if the Top hasn't negotiated the depth and breadth of the proposed scene with you, it's a pretty clear indication that this person has not yet taken BDSM 101. You might wish to ask more questions about their level of experience and also ask other people about this person. You might ask: "Sir/Ma'am, with respect, shall we spend some time planning this scene?"

Another suggestion for bottoms: If the Top has finished negotiating with you and failed to ask about your medical history as it could relate to the intended activities, I recommend that you reconsider what you are about to do. Although that person may have taken BDSM 101, they must have dozed off when this topic was discussed. Again, you might wish to ask more questions about their level of experience and also ask other people about this person. You might ask, "Sir/Ma'am, with respect, are there any medical conditions

---

Important note

Since subspace feels very much like being high—and since you lose touch with your own body when you are very high—bottoms sometimes get hurt because they cannot recognize that they are being hurt.

Playing when in an altered mental state can create a conflict within our community. Should the bottom get hurt, the community will find it hard to discern whether the bottom was hurt accidentally (perhaps because they couldn't communicate clearly with their Top) or whether the Top's actions were willful (the Top was a sadist using the bottom's altered state to play beyond the agreed-upon limits of the bottom's consent).

Nothing much comes of this when there are only isolated cases. Club officers and DMs watch for behavior patterns. Frankly, the bottoms, themselves, are sometimes unsure whether the hurt was accidental or purposeful.

On the other hand, lots of drama, innuendo, and serious repercussions begin to occur if a bottom is hurt during play and the Top does not take responsibility and apologize for it.

---

that would limit aspects of the play you are considering doing with me?"

While you'll learn more of these as you gain experience, here are a few examples of medical conditions and play limitations:

- *Prior psychological trauma, especially sexual trauma*: Some forms of psychological play (such as rape scenes or some kinds of humiliation play) can trigger a flashback—or possibly a psychotic episode.

- Heart condition with electrically-driven implants such a heart- assist pump, a defibrillator, or a pacemaker:
  - No electrical play of any kind. You **must** keep them **physically distant** from a violet wand when it's on (as in, not in the same room).
  - No heavy impact play to the upper left chest or the upper left back. This includes floggers as well as fist (rough body play).

- *Breath and carotid play*: don't do it, period. Risk = brain damage, death. And, you will have NO warning. Trust me: law enforcement authorities are not the least interested that you didn't mean to kill the person.

- *Claustrophobia*: avoid any restrictive play particularly that covers the face.

- *Dissociative Identity Disorder*: there is controversy over this one. The issue for a Top is this: you might get consent from one of the person's personalities but find that you're playing with a different personality who arrives during play and makes it very clear that they had *not* given consent. Or, you believe that you have an understanding with one person only to discover that you're really dealing with someone quite different who pops up in a stressed situation. For the bottom, just imagine a Top getting an adrenaline rush from Top space and having a different personality emerge... scary!

Note to the bottoms

You are responsible for knowing what a Top needs to know so tha
you will recognize it when a Top does something incompletely or
completely wrong. Yes, this means that you need to know about
negotiation topics before you start negotiating with someone.

Yes, this means that you should know safety details for each type
of sensation you want to experience.

If you want someone to cane you, flog you, or spank you, you
should know something about safety issues as they relate to
caning, flogging, and spanking.

If you want someone to tie you up, you should know quite a bit
about bondage safety issues, particularly about the potential for
bondage-induced nerve damage.

If you wish to experience fire on your body (one form of edgeplay),
you should learn enough about fire play to know the safety issues.

You are responsible for your own body.

**You have to take responsibility, ultimately, to make decisions
about play and about safeguarding your own physical,
psychological, and emotional health.**

**Talk is cheap. Some people will claim to know some skill in order
to get their hands on you (and into your panties)**

You are responsible for your own body.

Know which skills involve more risks than others

Some forms of SM play involve greater risk than others. Obviously. You can't really compare safety risks of spanking with safety risks of needle play and you can't really compare the safety risks of needle play with the safety risks of breath play.

In BDSM, **edgeplay** is a subjective term that is used in two quite different ways. On the personal level, edgeplay is anything that a person isn't too sure that they want to experience but—with some hesitation and fear/concern—are willing to try. In its more general meaning, edgeplay refers to activities that are considered to be pushing the edge of the traditional SSC creed; these activities are considered more appropriate when you're playing by RACK standards. Items on this partial list require specialized training and are potentially dangerous.

Potentially dangerous but manageable:

- fire play;
- knife play;
- rough body play;
- electrical play; and
- blood play, piercing, and unsafe sex practices (increased risk of spreading disease).

So dangerous as to be foolhardy (this is a **do-not-do-these-under-any-circumstances** list):

- gunplay;
- breath play (erotic asphyxiation); and
- carotid play.

A Dom wrote to me recently explaining that the edgeplay that he and his submissive enjoy is particularly dangerous and he wondered whether it would be possible for the two of them to prepare a legal document that would explain the kind of play they do and hold him harmless from damaging her. As I am not a lawyer, I sent the question on to my friend Jay Wiseman, a court-qualified BDSM expert witness and former law school professor.

In his note back to me, Jay observed, "There is no such thing as a precaution that will block any possibility of supposedly false accusations, and contracts/pre-nups regarding sex are void from the moment of their alleged creation, at least as regards the sex part. As to edgeplay, about all such 'contracts' will do is alert the prosecution that both parties knew that great bodily injury might result from the activity in question, and consent is not a defense to a BDSM activity that has the potential to cause great bodily injury and does so."

So, the answer is: No, you cannot get out of responsibility for damaging your partner even if they are a willing play participant.

Message to Tops and bottoms: Don't play beyond your skill level and find mentors who can train you both in the skill and the requisite safety requirements that are part of this kind of activity. I know, I've already said all this. Over and over.

Safety issues you must know

There are a few safety issues that Tops and bottoms **absolutely must know**. These are SM topics where the Top must study and/or have personal training; a Top can't *wing it* in these areas. Both the Top and bottom MUST know the safety rules for the specific type of play they're doing. For example:

- You must not bind someone when doing fire play (you can wrap their wrists around a rope that **they** are holding to make it look as though they are bound, but they, themselves, *must not* be bound);
- You must know the okay and not-okay strike zones for any form of impact play;
- You must know which lubes are intended for an anus, which lubes are intended for a vagina, and which lubes go (or don't go) with silicone or latex toys and why;

- If you are using wrist cuffs and attaching someone to a Saint Andrew's Cross for your flogging or whipping scene, you *must* use quick-release snaps in case they faint. You'll not be able to lift an unconscious person while at the same time unclipping their wrist cuffs. However, cautions Scott Smith, a nationally prominent rope suspension expert, you must use *full load quick-disconnect snaps* with an appropriate load-rating and safety factor. Scott recommends a load rating of 5:1 minimum and preferably greater than 15:1. He warns: "Please don't use tack-shop 'panic snaps' unless you really like paperwork."

- You must know the signs when someone has been suspended too long;

- Despite what you may think, *canes* are advanced implements, and you'll need some instruction;

- "More deaths and permanent damage results from bondage than from all other forms of modern BDSM play combined." (Jay Wiseman, author of *SM 101: A Realistic Introduction* and an expert witness on BDSM injuries);

- Compression (clothespins, for example) can create cell or nerve damage if left on too long. (Relevance? There is a risk of leaving them on too long because they don't hurt very much when they're on you. You do NOT want part of a breast, nipple, clit, or penis to permanently lose sensation);

- You must at least wear safety glasses when you begin to learn to throw a whip of any length. In addition to the safety goggles, please buy and wear a sombrero if you're going to learn how to throw a <u>bullwhip</u>. No, according to those who know about such things, a cowboy hat won't protect enough of your face (you won't think this advice to be so silly after you've tried to throw a bullwhip a time or two).

So, bottoms, you also must learn how to tell whether a specific Top is competent in a particular SM technique. Have you watched them play and asked others about them?

So, Tops, how can you tell if a bottom is a good candidate to be *your* bottom? How can you tell whether a possible play partner is exaggerating *their* experiences? How can you tell whether they are emotionally stable or unstable? The cold reality of it is that it may be hard within a small BDSM community to find someone who will be fully truthful with you, particularly if you are relatively new and they are more established. They don't know what you'll do with the honest answer. (You might repeat it. You might cause a lot of damage with the information.)

The more you learn, the happier and safer you'll be

A BDSM scene is a dance. Those of you who have gone dancing on a Friday night realize that most people on the dance floor are trying to wing it. They haven't taken lessons; they don't want to take lessons. Lessons aren't necessary; after all, how hard can it be to dance to music. *Dancing*, according to them, is about *fun* and lessons aren't fun.

But, then you see a few couples that have clearly had some lessons. They're better. Their movements are more interesting and the couples are working together to accomplish a common goal—to dance to the music. You're enjoying the show along with your beer. Then, one couple dances by and something causes you to watch them. They are fascinating; what they are doing is magical. You can't take your eyes off them. The leader is giving seemingly invisible signals that the follower seems to understand intuitively. They are going through dance moves and patterns you've only seen on TV. The gulf between your level of dance knowledge and their level of dance knowledge seems unbridgeable.

That is exactly what you are going to find as you advance in this world of BDSM.

You will go to a play party, and most of the people will seem to be muddling through. A couple is doing a spanking scene over here, a flogging scene over there, a bondage scene over there, a caning scene over there. A Top, using a flogger, whip, or cane is standing a few feet away from his bottom without much **connection**. The bottom is either writhing in agony or looking a little bored. Not many people are watching the scene; there is really no reason to watch it. Most of the scenes appear to be about the same.

And then you spot the crowd: Ten, 15, 20 people gathered 'round a couple to watch magic. To your surprise, it still appears to be a flogging, caning, or spanking scene much like the others—but somehow different. It's going to take you some time to figure out that difference.

Your reputation

Unlike the public impression, BDSM is a skills-based discipline where how much you know matters and how much you practice matters and how safe you play matters and how considerate you are of your partner matters. All of these go into the mix called your reputation.

You're on stage the minute you start a public scene; all those people watching will talk about you.

It will take you longer, still, to learn how to reliably create magic.

As with every skill, mastery comes with a price tag. To become a crowd-drawing magical BDSM player, you'll have to *do* certain things:

- read books (see Amazon's list of the 100 best-selling BDSM books: www.bdsmbooknews.com);
- watch DVD skills demos (e.g., search for *SMTech* on Amazon);
- go to LOTS of education programs at your local BDSM club;
- attend weekend kink conferences as often as you can. (see: www.thebdsmeventspage.com); and
- practice

And practice. And practice. Yes, you can be monogamous and practice only with your partner, but your learning may be slowed—just as it would be if you took dance lessons and declined to change partners during classes: your partner will learn to compensate for your weaknesses and you won't learn as quickly.

Not as simple as it sounded in *50 Shades of Gray*, is it?

All of which brings us back to the topic of this section: *The more you learn, the happier and safer you'll be.*

Some messages for Tops

Back to the *dance* analogy: Have you watched couples social dancing at your local nightclub or country western bar? Have you ever noticed that they're seldom *looking* at one another? The man is dancing, the woman is dancing, music is playing, their feet are moving, but their eyes are cold and they are not looking at one another. Their minds are a hundred miles away. Hold that thought and observe people playing at your next BDSM play party. In the same way that magical dancers are clearly emotionally connected, the magical BDSM players are clearly emotionally connected. The Top is constantly touching the bottom, constantly checking to make sure they are taking this trip together. **The Top is giving back to the bottom**. All of the Top's focus is on the bottom—not on what others think of the performance, not on how he looks throwing a flogger. Scenes and relationships are two-way streets.

Suggestion for Tops: Read Dossie Easton and Janet Hardy's *The New Topping Book*. It explains how to be a good Top.

Some messages for bottoms

Yes, the sensations are interesting—actually, they're marvelous. You feel as though you could just stand or lie there and play for hours. You're just soaking it all in. But are you a good bottom? Will this Top wish to play with you again? What are you giving back? Are you wiggling? Are you maintaining eye contact? Are you *connecting*?

Suggestion for bottoms: Read Janet Hardy and Dossie Easton's *The New Bottoming Book*. It will explain how to be a good bottom.

In 2007, a friend of mine named Graydancer wrote a brief piece titled "The art of Giving Back. *Most don't.*" He had become frustrated with bottoms simply *receiving* the Top's gifts, so he wrote this piece to provide a little guidance.

> "You are the person who makes the sounds, gives the touch, the wiggle, the tiny inclining of the head just to *touch in* those slight lulls in the scene. You are the person who makes eye contact—or breath contact or toe contact or hell, *aura* contact of some kind—during the scene, and lets your partner know that you are there with them. You are the person who, even in the midst of the most brutal beating, will give their ass just the slightest touch of acknowledgment at the gift you've been given. Or the sub who will kneel, bundled in a down coat and about to brave the Wisconsin snow, just for the chance to kiss the foot of the Dom who's just bound and tormented her."

Chapter 3
Finding Others

Exploring D/s Online

With its possibilities for online play, the Internet can be a useful aid for personal discovery. It's a safe way to begin to explore activities that actually excite you. Please keep in mind that textual play, while often exciting, doesn't transfer well to actual, BDSM-based relationships or safe SM play. Novels and media are intended primarily to titillate and only secondarily are meant to inform. However, everything that you learn—however you learn it—ultimately helps to point you in the direction of relationships and play that excites and interest you, so they all have their place.

Exploring your sexual kinkiness online has some advantages. Because you don't have to reveal your sexual preferences to someone sitting in front of you, you can avoid the mortifying situation where the person says, "Eww, you're weird," or some such. Although many people fear admitting that they have non-standard sexual tastes, you're likely to find communities online who share your preferences and who will welcome you warmly.

But let's name this for what it is: even if you're only coming out online, it is still a coming out that requires the kind of courage and tact that our brave gay friends have demonstrated when they've decided to live in authenticity and reveal their dreams and needs to family and friends. Coming out kinky is just as scary and delicate. Starting out online eases that transition.

While clearly beneficial in some ways, online D/s relationships are controversial within our community. For those involved, such relationships can become very real and intense—different from real-time relationships, but exciting and fulfilling in other ways. Sometimes these online long-distance relationships (LDRs) evolve into real-time (RT) relationships; sometimes an online couple will get together in RT only to discover that their actual personalities and behaviors are hugely different from what had been apparent through the online courtship.

Since the online D/s community is so large and growing so rapidly, I thought that I should provide some suggestions.

Online Safety

While you mostly hear about male <u>sexual</u> predators on the Internet, you sometimes *do* hear of women who cruise the Internet as <u>financial</u> predators. Here are some basic suggestions as you're looking for online relationships of any kind.

Who is this person, really? While you do know that online friends could actually be VERY different than they portray themselves, please raise your level of skepticism enough to engage your self-preservation instincts. The person with whom you're chatting—and even speaking to on the phone—is largely unverifiable. You usually don't know much about the person and you can't find out very much. They can represent themselves any way they wish. As with well-trained salesmen in any field, they can quickly identify your interests, fears, and motivations, then feed those back to you to make themselves appear to be the answer to your dreams. This reality casts a pall over online meetings.

Don't share personal information: Be *very* cautious about giving out any personal information, especially your home address, until you've established a solid level of confidence with your online friend. If the person simply *must* mail something to you, take out a Post Office box. If they continue to press for your address (or anything else), reread the section on red flags and be careful. (Along these lines, I assume that you wouldn't provide credit or debt card numbers, right? You won't offer to *help this person out financially* , right?)

Be careful about digital images: Don't send photos that you wouldn't put on your own Facebook page. Only send images that you'd show your folks or your employer.

TECHNOLOGY NOTE: These cautions particularly apply to using your webcam: if you wouldn't want your parents or boss seeing it on YouTube, don't do it on webcam—they're designed to record to your computer.

Trust, but verify: Ask yourself—are you taking this ride together or are you being taken for a ride? In statistics and in real life, you need a lot of data points in order to draw meaningful conclusions. It could take you months of online chatting to conclude whether or not your Internet friend is legitimate. Remember the Russian proverb: *Trust, but verify*. It's one thing if *they* tell you something; it's quite another thing if an independent source verifies that it's really true. So for your own safety, try to find an *independent, verifiable source* that will corroborate this person's accomplishments or personal history.

Don't disconnect your brain when you log on: Don't be bullied or cajoled into acting outside your comfort zone. "Bullied," you ask? Well… does your Internet-mate seem to need to feel powerful and in control? Do they seem to need to feel superior (e.g., telling you that you're doing something wrong and you practically never get it right)? Do you sense that they are ignoring your point of view and get angry with you for not doing exactly as they've instructed? Do they seem to enjoy hurting you psychologically? Well, those are all key characteristics of a bully.

Acting within your comfort zone also means that you recognize that much of what goes on over the Internet in BDSM chat rooms is fantasy play. You should rightfully become alarmed if someone starts referring to you as a "submissive" because you are a woman, or *requiring* you to call them Master, Mistress, Sir, or Ma'am (or referring to you as their Master/Mistress, submissive or slave) before the two of you have established your relationship parameters and negotiated how those titles and roles will be used—and what they mean for each of you.

Please remember one of the major lessons of this book: Words in BDSM mean different things to different people, and your understanding of those words changes as you gain knowledge and experience. So, while you're new to BDSM and playing with someone on the Internet, the two of you have to figure out what you mean by words such as *Master* or *slave*.

Honesty and integrity are transferable traits: Please be extremely cautious of those who make repeated excuses for keeping their online lives separate from their real-time partners. If they are unwilling to be honest with their significant other, why in the world would you think that they'll be honest with you?

Here's another true story: I know a woman whose husband forgot to turn off his computer screen when he left for work one day. Going to his desk to turn it off, she discovered his morning text message exchanges with a woman in another country. Reading them, she realized that after an 18-year marriage, her husband was about to divorce her and start a relationship with this other woman. Not a great way to start your morning.

Upon reading that story, PhoenixRed added: "I can't stress enough how much this happens online. I'm sure most participants in my online BDSM coaching rooms are filled with people whose real-time partners don't know what they are doing online. They say online that they love their online partner, but they have no intention of ever meeting their Dom or sub in real life. I'd guess that only a very small percentage of online relationships ever transition to RL. That percentage is bound to be even smaller for international relationships. Many online people cannot or will not do BDSM in real time."

Final reality check: Remember that you're really sitting in your own room with your own computer. You're alone; nobody has a gun to your head. If someone "orders" you to do something you feel is unreasonable, *just say no*. You can refuse to undress or perform sex acts in front of your webcam unless **you** think it's going to be hot to undress and perform sex acts while being broadcast. Just remember—since you don't know the person with whom you're interacting, you might as well assume that they are recording your chat and lying when denying it. Their ethical standards are both unknown and unknowable. The person who loves and protects you today may hate you and expose you tomorrow.

Long Distance Relationships (LDRs)

All right, safety aside, why spend time setting up an online long-distance relationship? Hmmm… it seems to me that some reasons for doing this are more valid and honest than others.

I can certainly understand spending time and effort establishing an online relationship if you live in an area where there is little or no safe real-time D/s community. I can also understand doing this if your life is too busy or your work/school hours are such that you just can't join the real-time community. I can also understand it if you simply are not interested in the nitty-gritty of an actual physical relationship and feel that an online LDR is just fine.

I can almost understand playing online if you want to pretend that you're someone other than who you are. Perhaps you would like to explore how you are treated being one age and gender and then how you are treated if you appear to be another age and gender. But, then *you* would be the one representing yourself dishonestly online, so how would you justify that to yourself? I can also almost understand playing online as you're adjusting to your own kinkiness and you want to get a sense of how others will react to you or it. But remember, what you may *think* is a private online existence may not be as private as you believe.

Now, I strongly recommend against developing an online LDR if you're already in a committed relationship—possibly married—and you're using the online experience to fulfill D/s needs your partner cannot (or will not) meet. An honest online LDR ethically requires that your significant other knows what you're doing and approves of it (or at least tolerates it). With or without sex, an online relationship is still a relationship and secrets are still secrets. Secrets destroy relationships. Anyway, you'll eventually be discovered.

Safety precautions aside, the Internet can be useful for meeting people. Many people have met kinky partners there. So long as you are aware of the red flag safety concerns and behave honorably and with integrity, you should be able to find many others with your interests and desires.

There is a counterpoint to the benefits of using the Internet to meet people and to socialize: you're playing on the Internet rather than going out to munches, club meetings, and parties. To be lucky and find a like-minded real time partner, you have to go out and be seen where others are looking for someone like you.

Moving from the Internet to *real time*

Once you start looking for real-time BDSM, you'll find a world full of munches, discussion groups, parties, and specialized conferences. There are many opportunities to learn stuff—and it should be easy to find experienced BDSMers willing to help you. Since you are reading this book, chances are that your BDSM interest is serious; you probably know quite a bit about the online world. There are only a few points to keep in mind as you move from fantasy to reality.

If your experience thus far has mainly been online, those whom you meet in real time may not credit you with much experience.

You're going to have to prove yourself to be a trustworthy and safe person; in this community, respect is earned, not assumed.

If you are a Top online, please find a competent mentor who can provide both skill and safety instruction as you learn to be a Top in real time. Please be aware, a Dom/me and a Top are two quite separate things. While playing as the Internet Dom/me, you doubtless did all kinds of deliciously wicked things to your sub(s), which is not a problem. However, your Topping experiences are not directly transferable. One cannot go from being an Internet whip master to whipping a real person. When you decide to try your new whip on some lovely (and very real) lady and your errant whip stroke takes a chunk of flesh from her back, "oops" may not get you a second date. Equally bad is what you're quite likely to do to yourself (and your ego) should you try that first whip strike without some coaching. (Remember, I've already given you one tip about learning how to throw a whip. Here's a second tip: learning how to throw a whip is not as easy as it looks. The crack that a whip makes means that the cracker—the piece of cord at the tip—exceeded the speed of sound, which is 768 mph at sea level. You'll not want the rebound hitting you.)

As you move from Internet to real time, please remember the rules of *safe, sane and consensual*; make sure you have your safewords sorted out. Take what you have learned online about domination, negotiating a scene, setting the mood, etc., and add two doses of watchfulness and humility. A little humility can be good: most of us have plenty to be humble about.

If you're considering taking your online relationship into a real time relationship, please be doubly cautious. You may scene wonderfully with a Dom/me or sub online, but may find that their dominance or submission affects you very differently in real time. They may not be prepared to do things in real time that they do online. Once again—*talk.* Then talk some more. In BDSM, communication is paramount, whether it's online or real time. By the way, if you are meeting someone in real time with whom you have been playing online, you each may be in for some surprises. Since chat room communication excludes voice intonation and subtext subtlety, the impression you have of this other person may differ from the impression they thought they were giving you.

Here's an extreme case that happened recently to the best friend of one of my close friends. This 20-something woman developed an online relationship with a man. The relationship grew and grew.

After a few months (yet without ever meeting), he invited her to move in with him; he offered to pay for her flight. Believing that her dreams had come true, she gave away her cherished dog, gave up her apartment, put all her belongings in storage, and moved from Austin, Texas, to Stockholm, Sweden. He paid for everything, including her return trip three weeks later. She was not what he had expected. She didn't get her dog back.

Bringing your online relationship into real time risks ruining a good friendship. Your real-time relationship may fail because the levels of intimacy involved online cannot be replicated in real time. Said differently, your online friend may be quite different in person. Online, anyone can be anyone.

Using the Internet to find people and clubs

While I've included a few website suggestions in Supplement B, my strongest suggestion is to join FetLife.com. It's a free social-networking website—the kinksters' version of Facebook. Here, you can find like- minded others in your own community (or in almost any community in the world) by searching for the name of your city. Not only will your search produce a list of kinky folks who live in or near that city, but when you scroll down, you'll see whether any Fetlife group has that city's name in its title.

Speaking of FetLife groups, you'll be able to fin specialty groups interested in a wide variety of topics; you can look up answers to common questions or pose your own questions and get a multitude of replies. Here, you can learn when most of the large BDSM events will take place anywhere in the country, if not the world.

FetLife can be a big help when trying to find out about a prospective play partner—or even just a prospective friend. You can read about their likes and dislikes, see what groups they belong to, and see whether you have friends in common. In a general way, the more information on someone's Fet page, the better. While recognizing that all of us had to start on Fet at one time or another, when you find a Fet profile that is essentially empty and they have few (or no) friends, you should be cautious. Sure, this person may be new to BDSM and has just joined FetLife. Or, there may be some other reason.

Beyond using FetLife to search for BDSM clubs in your city, you might conduct an Internet search using the search phrase *information BDSM* along with the name of the nearest big city. If that doesn't work, try *munch BDSM* with the city name. So long as you are near a reasonably large city, you're likely to find something—although a FetLife search would be a lot more efficient. As small towns generally don't have many or any BDSM clubs/events, be prepared to have to travel to a larger city to find like-minded people. (NOTE: if you try to search using only *BDSM* rather than *information BDSM* or *munch BDSM* you'll end up with a bunch of porn sites.)

If possible, use FetLife to find a member of a local club who can accompany you to your first munch and introduce you to club members. You can also ask them when to show up and what to wear (casual clothes; nothing that screams out, "I'm weird as hell and can't believe I've finally found others who are the same as me!").

Typically, clubs hold three kinds of events: munches, education meetings, and play parties. Some clubs are known mostly as party clubs; some clubs are known for their education programs; some smaller communities only have munches. The direction a club takes depends upon the members' interests and the leaders' commitment to educating those members. Because clubs have different nuances, you may wish to participate in all that are available until you find those that seem best to fit you

Going to a *munch*

A **munch** is a casual social gathering where newcomers can meet some established club members without the pressure of showing up at a BDSM club meeting. Munches are usually held at a restaurant—often in a private room of that restaurant. While primarily a time for like-minded friends to socialize, some munches also include announcements from local organizations. You can come and go within the specified hours. There are no dress codes and there is no BDSM play. Some munches may be restricted to a specific group, such as women or submissives, but they're the exceptions, not the rule.

While it's natural to be concerned about what to wear and whether or not you'll fit in, he almost universal answers are:

- Don't worry too much about what you wear.
- People are people, so the way that you are welcomed at a BDSM get-together will feel about the same as being the new person joining any group of people who already know one another. Awkward, at the very worst.
- If the munch (or club, for that matter) contains turf-guarding (or newbie-cruising) Doms, it may be uncomfortable. On the other hand, if the club leadership actively reaches out to new members, then they'll make sure that the munch and club experiences are warm and welcoming. Remember that *first impressions* are lasting impressions and people only get one chance to get a first impression of you. Smile and don't volunteer a lot of information at first

Here are some pre-munch suggestions:

- You should be honest about your interest in such things as protocols, rituals, structure, and such, as these are pretty common discussion topics (since you're reading this book, you're going to know quite a bit about these topics).
- If you are a woman, you should be prepared for many of the dominants in the room to make the shallow assumption that because you are female, you are (therefore) submissive. This

is particularly true if you show up with a man—even if he's actually a submissive man. I agree with PhoenixRed who suggests that your first line of defense is to smile and reply that you're on the other side of the slash (referring to the "/" line between D and s) and that you're not submissive. Unfortunately, some dominant men have trouble believing that a woman even *can* be a Domme and will continue to push you. You may have to discuss this with a club office . If this person *is* a club office , then your own sense of tact and strategy will have to guide you.

- If you are a man, you should be prepared to meet some dominant women—FemmeDoms, or Dommes. They won't have signs around their necks, so treat everyone with the respect you hoped you, yourself, would receive.

- Your personal presentation will influence their impressions of you. This includes your dress and bearing, your ability to carry on a lucid conversation, and your table manners.

- *Doormats* attract abusers. Coming across as too eager to please often signals *desperation* rather than, say, *Southern hospitality* (assumptions, again). Most people are interested in speaking with people who are interesting. *Shyness* is sometimes confused with *aloofness*. How you appear (strong, confident, and knowledgeable or weak, withdrawn, and fairly clueless) will be taken in and interpreted through the filters of those that will befriend you. Their judgments of you will—in turn—affect your experience of that local BDSM club—at least until you become better known.

- We are all equals until we agree to some form of power exchange. If someone starts to Dom you upon first meeting, they've just unfurled a huge red flag. (Should this ever happen, I'll bet you'll find people watching you to see how you'll react. Remember what I mentioned earlier: It may take years for some people to pass out of the *asshole* stage, and some never do.)

- Most munches are welcoming places for new folk and a great way to get oriented in a new environment. That said, when you ask those new to BDSM about their first munch or club meeting, they frequently admit that they ended up sitting in their cars for a long time to work up the courage to walk through the door. Please be assured, we're all just people and we've all had to walk through that door the first time. Put on a big smile and go for it; it's not nearly as scary as you're imagining.

The first time I ever went to a club meeting (2001), it began with a pre-meeting social in a vanilla restaurant. This was a Leather club, not a BDSM club but I didn't know the difference at the time. There were a few people standing around talking who clearly did not look like any of the other patrons in the place. One man was stocky at about 5'10" and shaved bald. The other man was really a mountain in disguise— about 6'3" and 300 pounds of biker muscle—also shaved bald. The woman with him was big-boned and about 6' in her own right. All three of them were wearing black leather motorcycle jackets, Levi's, and spit-shined combat boots. They were leaning against the bar; they were not smiling. I was easily 20 years older than any of them and only 5'4" tall at about 130 pounds—my then-wife was 5' at 110 pounds; we looked at one another and said, "I guess that's the group!" So relax, it can't get much more intimidating than that!

Assessing the club

Most local BDSM clubs are fabulous; some are less than fabulous. Fortunately, those that are less good get fixed or go away over time. Unfortunately, some that are fabulous under their current leadership become less fabulous under successive leadership; over time, either the club goes away or you do. It's a roll of the dice; people are people and organizations go through various phases depending on the leaders.

You want a club that is stable—but until you know a thing or two about the club, it will be hard to assess its stability. Consider some of the following topics.

Friendliness: Are the established members open and welcoming? When you go to a meeting, do you feel welcome? Do people mix? Do established members come up and socialize with you because you're new? Do the leaders introduce you as a newcomer and spend time with you? Do most of the club members demonstrate respect for those just starting out? ... or are you fresh meat?

When I was first exploring BDSM clubs in Austin, I had two very different experiences within a few weeks of each other. At one club's munch, I was completely ignored, while at a different club's munch, I was openly welcomed. I was 56 at the time, and my own social behavior didn't change much in the intervening few weeks. Clubs differ—it's a matter of leadership.

Safety: Is the club, itself, a safe place? What's the tone of the club members' posts on their eGroup or on their FetGroup? You can often get an inside look at the club and its members by reviewing older posts. Are the posts positive and pleasant, or do you find flaming and name-calling? Importantly, if someone posts an opinion or point of view, are there people within the club who post hostile replies that vilify or publicly humiliate the *person* for having expressed their opinion? Be *very* careful of those being so negative to another's opinion; you probably should also be cautious about the club as a whole for tolerating someone who publicly humiliates someone for their opinion.

Hidden agendas: Some clubs are more predatory towards single women than others. In some clubs, established Doms work together informally to try to pick up the new subs—because it's a lot of fun to be the first person to give *that special experience* to a newbie.

Some clubs are actually *created* because a Dom wanted to establish himself as a *someone* and have access to attractive newbies.

In some larger and more established clubs, some of the senior submissives may develop their own network and work to ensure that new submissives get the *correct* information about Dom/mes in the community. While this sounds great in theory, it works less well when the senior submissives use their powers against people they simply don't like—as opposed to people who are unsafe or of low integrity.

Operations: Does the club run smoothly? Do members support one another or is there controversy about some of the club leaders? Have most of the members remained with the club over the past five years, or does the club have a history of people leaving to form their own splinter clubs? Ask around.

Here are other thoughts on the topic:

- Do people speak well of others in the club or is there a tendency to point out differences?

- When you're new to the club, do they assign an established member to help to answer your questions or do they exhibit predatory behavior toward new members? Do they have Dungeon Monitors at their parties (e.g., are they safe players)? How do they deal with unsafe players? Do they approach them with respect and treat their lack of safety as a lack of training, or are they accusatory, blaming them for not knowing something? How do they deal with someone who bristles at being corrected for unsafe play? Does the club have a policy of warning other club members of an unsafe player? What if the unsafe player is a senior member of that club?

- Are established dominants pleasant or unpleasant to a new Dom/me? Do they welcome the new Dom/me as a valuable potential resource or as a possible threat to the club's power balance?

- Are their officers primarily made up of members of the "in" crowd (retaining power year after year and blocking new people and/or new ideas)?

- Do they have a well-developed education component to their club meetings?

Stuff like that.

I realize that you can't answer such questions when you're just starting out; now you know the kinds of questions to be asking.

Becoming a good BDSM citizen

Rose is a good friend in Austin who owns and runs *Voyagers*, one of Austin's largest BDSM groups. For over a decade, she has held monthly education meetings and play parties in her home. She wrote a FetLife post last year after an upset (at one of her monthly parties) that sprang from gossip and rumors and started to grow in ways that threatened to impact the personal reputations of a few of the party attendees. I thought her post to be so succinct and well thought-out that I asked her to write down some guidelines for a personal code of conduct that I could include in this book. Rose agreed, and I'm including her observations and ideas here. I've adapted the following material to fit the tone/voice of this book. Please consider the remainder of this section to be hers.

Your inner journey: People know you by what you say and how you act. Often, the dividing line between being poorly thought of or well thought of is quite thin. There are some simple and straightforward filters that you can adopt that can help to keep you on the safe side of that line. To become known as a thoughtful person—a person of merit—in the eyes of those who listen to you and read your writings, you might consider establishing three guidelines as a personal *practice* (not merely as a *goal*).

- Ask yourself: *Do I know that what I'm saying is true?* If you don't know it's true for certain, wait to speak until you've found the truth.
- Ask yourself: *Do I feel that it is kind?* If you don't feel it's kind, find a better way of saying it.
- Ask yourself: *Do I believe that it's meaningful?* If you don't believe it's meaningful, look into yourself to discover why you're speaking without purpose.

For the last question, there are several words that can be used successfully along with the word *meaningful*. You could ask: Is it useful? Is it helpful? Only you can know which word resonates with you the most powerfully. Use that word, or find one that works for you. I've found that guidelines like these work best when they are adapted thoughtfully to one's personal vision.

Your frame of mind: The second part of Rose's advice is to make sure that the following statements are true of all your communication:

- I spread *gossip* only about joyful things;
- I speak about people I know as though I like them;
- I speak about the places I go as though I appreciate that they exist;
- I speak about the community as though I am a part of something that lifts me up; and
- I act as though our community is filled with people who are different from me, but no less worthy of consideration than I am.

Quoting directly, Rose concluded: "I encourage you to write your own statements. That way, they will resonate with you and you will be able to address topics and attitudes that are important to you that I didn't include here. While this advice is simple, we all know how challenging it can be to change established habits— particularly patterns of thought and speech that come to us as second nature.

"To encourage you, I want to leave you with a thought about how your life and your world might be improved by following the advice of Mahatma Gandhi who said, 'Be the change you wish to see in the world.' If you want the world to change, change yourself first. Even if you can't start applying this advice today, find some other good advice (or write your own!) and follow it." (This is the end of Rose's section.)

Finding a mentor

Mentoring means different things to different people. You might seek mentoring to help you integrate with your local club or you might seek someone to help you learn particular skills (e.g., flogging, rope ties, electrical stimulation). As you get further into our culture, you might seek someone to mentor you in protocols of some kind, such as tea service or formal dining (yes, all kinds of unexpected fetishes thrive well in here).

Some mentoring is quick, some take years. The more you appear to be thirsting for knowledge, the easier it will be to find a mentor. Limiting your request to a specific topic also increases your chance of finding a mentor. Have patience and keep looking until you find someone qualified to teach you what you want to learn—move on to something else until you can find a suitable teacher. *Waiting for the right time* is an important aspect of self-mastery. Self-mastery is an important aspect of your personality that others will consider as they assess your readiness for a mentor.

Before I leave this topic, a word of caution. *Mentoring is* sometimes used as a disguise for more established BDSMers to find still-naïve BDSM playmates. After all, those just starting out in BDSM are *fresh meat* to some more established players. Introducing a newcomer to BDSM is comparable to introducing a virgin to sexual play; it can be a lot of good fun.

Mentoring and BDSM

"A mentor is someone that guides and advises a newbie on what to expect, things they might want to learn, and other items. I believe a mentor should be on the same level as you. If you are submissive, then you should have a submissive mentor. Vise versa for a Dominant. They will be able to connect more with what you are thinking and feeling and can help you better than the opposing role could."

—*lunaKM*, Submissive Guide)

PhoenixRed comments that in addition to this somewhat-harmless risk for newcomers, there is a greater risk that predators are also lurking about from time to time trying to find young ones to use and abuse until their thirst is quenched or until the mentee/apprentice figures out that what they're going through is not what should be happening. Unfortunately, by then the predator has often ensnared this person in a web of emotional and psychological fears and insecurities. Breaking free from a predatory mentor can be emotionally and psychologically traumatizing, particularly if the person feels that they have been used. In extreme cases, someone who has gone through this cycle will be left with a sense of loathing about a world they once looked upon with such promise.

But, there are fairly easy ways to avoid this trap and the fact that you're reading this book gives you an immense edge over others new to this world.

In a Blog Post on *ThirstForBDSMKnowledge.blogspot.com* (November 22, 2008), Geoff W (writing there and on several other online sites as Evil_Geoff) explained a mentor's role in exquisite language. Since I couldn't have said this better, I've included it here—with his permission:

"**Mentoring Rules** by Geoff W. (Evil_Geoff): A mentor is a teacher, your guide, a sounding board, a friend. According to *Webster's*, a mentor is 'a trusted counselor or guide.' A mentor is there to answer your questions, offer advice, and point you in the direction to fin the answers you need. They are there to warn you when you are about to screw up... but they are **not** there to save you from your own hormones or stupidity.

"The Rules:

- "Rule #1: If they want to have sex with you, *they are not a mentor.*
- "Rule #1a: If you want to have sex with them, *you aren't looking for a mentor.*
- "Rule #2: If they want to play with you, *they are not a mentor.*

- "Rule #2a: If you want them to play with you, *you aren't looking for a mentor*.
- "Rule #3: If they try to run your life or deny you access to people or information to help you learn, *they are not a mentor*.
- "Rule #3a: If you are looking for them to run your life, make decisions for you, tell you who you can see, or what you can read, or who you can talk to in order to learn about this subculture, *you aren't looking for a mentor*.
- "Rule #4: *You*, and only *you*, are responsible for wisely choosing a mentor. *Do your effing homework* before asking someone to be a mentor for you.

"A mentor isn't a fuck-buddy, a friend with benefits, a play partner, or control freak for your life. Do not let a predator in mentor's clothing attempt to use you."

As lunaKM pointed out some years ago in an article she wrote for her eZine *Submissive Guide*: "Some people will cite their many years of participating in the BDSM community as part of their mentoring credentials. I have a bias that I will put on the table concerning a person's level of experience: I have met people with five years of BDSM experience who have learned a great deal. However, I have also met other people with five years of BDSM experience who seem to have learned very little—it's as though they've had one year of experience repeated five times. The challenge for you—Dom, Domme, sub, or Martian—is to learn enough to be able to discern the quality of someone's experience in this way of life before you ask them to lead you through some mentoring process."

Chapter 4
Doing This Safely

> *Doing things safely* applies to everything we do, whether we cross the street (wait for green), drive a car (seatbelt, check the mirror), or prepare food. We do these things safely by automation and routine. The trick is to learn what you need to learn in order to be safe. That's this chapter.

Safely meeting others—*safe-calls*

This is a section about self-preservation. This is a section about "an ounce of prevention is worth a pound of cure." This is a section about not being dangerously stupid. I know *many* Doms who use safe-call procedures on first dates. The e are some nutty subs out there, too.

Because you can't tell someone's real intent or truthfulness from online chatting—or even from casual contact within the BDSM community— this system has been developed to weed out the crazies even *before* your hot date.

A safe-call is a prearranged agreement with an outside party to keep track of you when you're on a BDSM date. Their job is to sound an alarm to get help if they don't hear from you by a particular time, using a particular code or signal. You should use a safe-call system any time you are planning a first meeting with someone—and possibly for second or third meeting as well.

Whenever you use a safe-call, be sure that the person you intend to meet knows that you are using this procedure. If they continue to want to meet you, they've just passed the first hurdle. Anyway, you *have* to let the other person know you're using safe-call procedures because it would be impolite suddenly to say: "Excuse me, I have to make my safe-call right now."

Safe-calls create a sense of dual accountability: both you and the person you're meeting have to make sure that someone's phone is charged, that you're not too drunk to make the call, and that you know what time it is. You may even bond over the shared task.

What if I'm so new that I don't have a safe-call friend?
There is an evolving national network of volunteers who will serve as your safe-call monitor. See nationalsafecallnetwork.org. You can also type "safe-call" in to www.FetLife.com and probably find someone. Best, of course, is to make some friends to serve as your safe-call buddies before going out on a BDSM date. Really, come present. Don't go out on a BDSM date until you know someone well enough to serve as your safe-call buddy.

Why use a safe-call system?

A safe-call has a number of uses, some more obvious than others. On the obvious side, if you get into trouble, somebody knows where you are and can alert authorities. By the way, a person who knows that you intend to use safe-call techniques will almost by definition be a safe person. This is because a predator won't wish to risk detection, and when you demonstrate that you are using safe-call techniques, you are communicating that you realize that there are risks in meeting someone with unknown and probably

opening rituals and safe-calls

A personal story from PhoenixRed: "I found that many or most male subs are very quick to offer their phone number and to meet—without taking many (if any) precautions. For an opening ritual, I've had them strip and inspect them—which they like—then I've cuffed their wrists and ankles, had them kneel, and hooked the ankles to a spreader bar. I then cuffed their hands behind their back and told them to try to get out of that position and out of the cuffs. They couldn't, of course.

Then, I would take out my very sharp 11-inch play knife and whisper in their ear, 'Does anyone know where you are or who you're with?' Most times, the answer was, 'No, Ma'am.' I then dragged the knife up their chest and whispered: 'You didn't want to know much about me before you came here, do you understand that once you are bound, I literally have your life in my hands?' After a pause to let that soak in, I go on to ask, 'How do you know I'm not batshit crazy and really want to hurt you?' That's when their eyes get very wide and they'd start struggling. I'd shush them and whisper: 'Well, you're lucky I'm not batshit nuts. You'd best be more careful if you go out to play with someone else you don't know well, though.'

Most men think they are physically more powerful than women and therefore believe that they can take back control at any point in a scene. I prove to them that is not the case. Hope they took more precautions after that."

- PhoenixRed

Safe-calls—Two Critical Elements

Be sure that the person you're meeting knows that you are using safe-call procedures.

Be sure you and your safe-call partner are very clear about when to sound an alarm and specifically what to do if you don't check in on time or if you don't use the correct I'm safe code.

unusual sex practices. This applies equally to men or women new to BDSM who are going out on a first (or second) date.

On the less obvious side, your own credentials are improved in the eyes of an experienced BDSMer. They will recognize that you have done your homework, acted upon what you learned, and are a good candidate to be a safe player.

How does it work?

A good safe-call is one in which your contact person (someone you know to be both reliable and capable of making good decisions) has as much information as possible about your planned meeting. They need to know:

- time and date of meeting;
- your full name, home
- address, phone numbers (home and cell, if possible), and details about your car (make, model, and license plate number);
- all the same information about the person you're planning on meeting *plus*:
  - ○ Online ID, how you met them, and any other information you have about them, including any references you were able to obtain.
  - ○ Physical description of the person—age, phone number, etc., and
  - ○ The address and phone number where you will be

meeting and/or playing and the *type* of location (home, restaurant, etc.). (Please don't play privately on your first meeting; you must establish *trust* before entrusting your body to somebody.)

- ° It would be nice if you could get a copy of their drivers' license, but because of concerns about identity theft, that's probably not going to happen.

In addition, your safe-call person needs to know:

- any special details about the meeting that you've considered any special details about the meeting that you've considered ("If he/she is really hot, maybe I'll get laid!");
- the *emergency signal* that you'll use ("No, I won't be out too late—I'll sleep in on the weekend" could work.);
- when the safe-calls are to be made... (These are the typical times; yours have to fit he situation...):
  - ° when the person first arrives and you have just sat down together;
  - ° that you're okay according to some schedule—such as every hour on the hour with only five minutes of grace period;
  - ° as soon as the meeting is over and they have left; and
  - ° once you have arrived home safely.
- the conditions that would cause them to contact law enforcement authorities. (The police are not going to think it's funny if they go out looking for you only to find that you fell into lust, left your phone in your car, and hopped into someone's bed; it's likely to dampen their enthusiasm to follow-up on future safe-call cries for help from others.)

Your safe-call person needs to know the specific non-obvious phrase(s) you'll be using to indicate your status. Because this is the key to the process, I'll give you a solid example.

Example of safe-call banter that confirms your status:

"While you may think that it's the most major buzz kill on Earth to have to explain to your potential date that you will be using safe-call procedures, it's something that can be explained through e-mail before you meet. A safe-call is a good test to see whether your date is actually interested in your safety; most experienced BDSMers on a date with a relative newcomer will remind them to make (or take) their safe-calls."

– PhoenixRed

This example centers your conversation about a fictitious pet that has become ill that day. Since your date can only hear your side of the conversation, you're free to speak in code:

- "Hey, is Fluffy okay? She just didn't seem very perky today. You sure? Well okay, then. Please keep an eye on her, though," translates as: "I'm okay."

- "Fluffy **is** acting funny? What do you mean? (Pause and listen.) "Oh, okay, I've seen her do that. All right, thanks. I'll call you in half an hour to check on her," translates as: "I'm not too sure about this person; please stand by."

- "What! Fluffy threw up? OMG! I'll be right home!" is your obvious escape path.

Example of using a single word to confirm that you are completely comfortable with your date:

- "Oh, you don't need to stay up. Just get in your **pajamas** and go on to bed."

Final (and perhaps paranoid) notes about safe-call technique

I suggest that you meet for the first time at a restaurant that has multiple closed-circuit TV cameras watching the room (such as IHOP™). If you feel threatened, you can mention these cameras (As in, "Wow! This place even monitors the dining room with video cameras! What do you think they're looking for?").

I urge you to play in a public party for the first few times. Don't go to a private house/apartment. As you're exploring our world, you'll want supportive people around who can monitor the play. Also, public play demonstrates through action that your play partner is legit and an accepted community member. It also gives you an opportunity to observe people's reactions to him/ her.

Now, the first time you agree to play with someone in *private*, don't permit the Top to do anything that may prevent you from escaping. This means that you should drive your own car to the Top's place so you can leave when you choose. It also means no bondage activities until you've had a few confidence-building scenes. Remember: in this culture, trust is earned, not given. You have all the time in the world to explore BDSM; there are lots of play partners out there. Your chances of being hurt decrease dramatically if you're being careful.

Please be careful about sharing your phone number: smart phones capture the number and it is then pretty easy to obtain your name and address. You're not going to want to pick up a stalker. Alternatives: block your outgoing phone number or use an Internet-based phone service (they can't be traced back to a physical location), or require people you don't know to e-mail you (you can set up a special e-mail account just for this purpose). By the way, my former Owner would not reply to an initial e-mail from a man unless the sender could obtain an introduction from someone she knew.

Physical safety in play

Often, your job is to take your bottom outside their comfort zone and to bring them back safely. While they're not here to go on the kiddy ride, they're also not here to be used as an experimental test subject while the Top is learning a new edgy skill.

Jay Wiseman (author of many books, including *SM-101: A Realistic Introduction*) currently serves as an expert witness in BDSM-related cases that are heading to trial. We have been friends for many years. Over lunch one time, he mentioned that the number-one indicator that a scene is about to go wrong occurs when the Top turns and says, "Now, watch this!"

Play scenes can be risky under the best of situations; they can be catastrophic under the worst of situations. Let's take a look ...

Establishing limits

If you think that you **do not** want to try some proposed SM experience, you have two choices: don't try it (yet) or find a trustworthy senior Top who can be relied upon to lead you gently as far through the experience as you choose. While you may be afraid of fire or of being whipped or be squeamish around needles, it's very likely that your actual experience of these sensations will differ from your imagined experience of them.

Remember, this is not the vanilla world where what you see is what you get. Here, things can be different than they appear. While I certainly encourage you to establish limits about the *kinds* and *intensity* of the activities that you permit others to perform on your body, I also encourage you to find people qualified to safely give you experiences that you will find nowhere else in life.

Violated boundaries or limits: From a technically legal point of view, if you're playing by SSC rules (as opposed to RACK rules) and the bottom calls *red* and the Top fails to stop whatever it is that is being done, the Top is committing *battery in* most states of the U.S. and the bottom can report that to the police. While this is true in theory, there are some reasons this is seldom done in practice.

- The bottom is embarrassed that they couldn't take the intense sensations—thus turning the blame inward instead of toward the Top who unethically played through the red. (This is tied to the lack of understanding about the appropriate use of—or response to the use of—colors in play.)
- The bottom may view this as a one-of-a-kind situation, hoping it doesn't happen again. (Some people prefer not

to recognize a situation for what it really is: this state is sometimes called, *floating on the River of deNial* or *playing Queen of deNial.*)

- The bottom may consider the Top to be a Senior Dom/me who was simply pushing their limits and the scene got a little out-of- hand. (Yeah, right.)

- The Top has threatened to expose them to their workplace, to their family, or in other ways to intimidate them if they say anything negative about the Top or the way the Top handled the scene. (This situation occurs occasionally within our community; as each situation is different, you may wish to consult the National Coalition for Sexual Freedom— NCSF— about actions you might pursue. Almost without exception, you are dealing with the criminal actions of a predator who has a history of behaving just this way. It is usually very difficult to stop such a person because of the hold they have established over you. Translation: They will blackmail you by threatening to "out" you if you say anything. This is the dark underbelly of BDSM and it's extremely difficult to separate fact from the "he said, she said" loop to affix actual blame.

Message to bottoms: Calling *red* is definitely touchy for a Top, and the situation is frequently made worse by new bottoms who call *red* to control a scene. This is called *Topping from the bottom.* If they do this often enough, it becomes the BDSM equivalent of crying wolf, and Tops will grow to distrust them. Yes, it's important for bottoms to call *red* when they need to, but the accepted practice is to call *yellow* long before it gets to the *red* point.

Correctly using safewords

When it comes to using safewords, there is a bit of a secret code. While calling *red* after calling *yellow* a time or two certainly communicates to the Top that the bottom has reached their limits for the night, that is **not** usually the conclusion the Top will draw when the bottom calls *red* with no prior warning.

If the bottom calls *red* as the scene is beginning, it usually is taken to mean that something is **physically** wrong (circulation constriction, dehydration, etc.) and doesn't necessarily mean the scene stops for the night. Under these conditions, a bottom suddenly calling *red* means that the Top is to stop, consult with the bottom to discover the problem, and then decide whether or not it can be fixed. A suggestion: If something is physically wrong, call out what is wrong rather than calling *red*. So—if your shoulder is binding up, call out *shoulder*; if there is a knot hurting your back, call out *knot in my back*.

We've discussed how the bottom may end a scene by calling *red*. Tops can end a scene, too.

These are some other reasons why a Top may end a scene early:

- A Top may decide to terminate a scene that has just begun if the bottom calls *red* during the warm-up stage on the grounds that this bottom is just not prepared for this Top's kind of scene. Something must not have been clear at the negotiations stage, so the scene should stop. This makes sense.

- A Top may feel that the bottom is trying to control the scene by calling colors inappropriately. This is an example of *Topping from the bottom*, and can push a Top to stop the scene in disgust.

- A Top may decide to terminate a scene that has just begun upon triggering a psychological landmine.

Message to bottoms: The Top has to trust that you will use a safeword for the right reasons, not as a way to manipulate the scene. Remember, those watching the scene are expected to recognize and to act when a *red* is called. Those watching don't understand if you call *red* only needing to be repositioned on the spanking bench—they only know that you called *red*, yet the play continued. Not great.

Message to Tops: your reputation is based on your word; your word and your actions establish the community's trust in you as a person. If your bottom calls *red*, stop immediately. So long as you are playing by SSC rules, there are *no exceptions*.

When safeword signals simply will not work

There are times during play—for example, when bound and gagged—when the bottom will be unable to speak but will be fully conscious. As an alternative, you can use a brightly colored ball or small bell (or even crumpled-up bit of tin foil) as physical backups for safewords. The bottom can drop the item as a signal that you need to check in. Dropping the item may signal either *red* or *yellow* and you'll have to go up to the bottom to determine which it is.

Bear in mind that if you are playing in a dungeon or other noisy place, it may be hard to see or hear a dropped item. Consider that when you're selecting the item that the bottom will be holding.

Safewords such as *red* and *yellow* won't work for bottoms in subspace: They aren't likely to realize that they're being hurt. Most people in subspace become detached from their bodies; they become disoriented and wrapped up in the sensations they're experiencing in

Playing through red

Playing through red is a very touchy point. If a Top plays through red in a public play party, it can lead to a huge uproar within a community. I know a senior Dom who had been at a BDSM conference in another state. He watched a play party scene where a Top played through red. By the time he got back to Austin, his inaction was being discussed very negatively on three of our local BDSM eGroups—despite the fact that there were DMs at that party that did not intervene and this Dom had no official role whatsoever. We are a very safety-conscious community.

their own private, emotional world. Once a bottom has reached this dreamy condition, coming out of their emotional state and back into their thinking state enough to realize that they need to call a color requires them to break the scene. But, because they're drifting in subspace, they don't realize there is any

Responsibility

It is completely the Top's responsibility to be able to read the bottom's physical and emotional conditions in order to give them a good, safe ride. It is completely the bottom's responsibility to give verbal and non-verbal signs and signals that are clear enough for the Top to read. Again, I recommend both The Topping Book and The Bottoming Book by Janet W. Hardy and Dossie Easton. Those books will make this paragraph real.

Now, let's say that the bottom doesn't call red. Let's say the scene goes bad. This is the point at which boys are separated from men, girls from women. Since scene safety is completely the Top's responsibility, it is both unethical and unbelievable (as in, nobody will believe them) for a Top to try to avoid personal responsibility for a scene going bad by blaming the bottom for not calling a color. The Top simply cannot get away with saying something like, "Well, you didn't use your safeword," or "Why didn't you say something?"

As a Top, your personal honor, integrity, and reputation can well hinge on times like these: Do you or do you not respect the bottom's feelings? Do you or do you not recognize your role in the mishap and learn from it for future practice?

need for that (a catch-22). In fact, at this stage in most scenes, the bottom is *flying* and asking for *more, harder, faster*... The bottom isn't thinking of consequences, the bottom is thinking, "Oh fuck oh fuck oh fuck oh fuck."

However... if an unskilled Top applies a sensation that is too intense or too disharmonious with the play pattern, the bottom **is** likely to snap out of their emotional space and back into headspace—at which point they probably *are* capable of calling a color. (Frankly, they're more likely to cuss you out before they can figure out that they should call a color.)

The Top's ability to read a bottom is a function of the Top's training and experience in BDSM play. A bottom will have to watch a Top play with other bottoms in order to assess that Top's skill level. For this reason, before permitting that Top to play with them, BDSM newcomers are urged to attend play parties—and speak with other bottoms with whom that particular Top has played.

By the way, just because Top A is skilled at activity X does not mean that they know squat about activity Y. Just because the Top can do a good flogging doesn't mean they can do a good caning. I've been to a lot of big play parties, and it's been my experience that while Tops with fewer than 4-5 years of experience manage to become okay (but not great) at a few skills, those Tops who become spectacular have gone out of their way to obtain advanced training... and they have practiced a lot.

This brings me back to the topic of this entire section: physical safety in play. One of the great risks with new Tops is that they *think* they know what they're doing because nobody corrects them. A similar situation can occur when people attribute *skill-knowledge* to someone who has been in the scene 5+ years without watching them play. That's what makes them risky. As I've already said, some people with five years of BDSM experience have experienced continuous growth and learning and know a lot; other people simply became five years older.

Contingency planning

Recently, Jen and I were presenting in Dallas when one of the participants mentioned that he had worked out a system so first-responders could understand/interpret the scene should something happen to *him* while his play partner was also bound or, in his words, "should an airplane crash into the house and the police stumble upon the scene." With permission from Sh3ph3rd (his FetLife username) here is his explanation:

> "When negotiating a scene, I always use ICE cards ['In Case of Emergency' cards]. They are nothing special, just orange or green 3x5 index cards that can be purchased at any discount store. On the back of the card is written the SCENE NAME in bold letters. On the front side (the lined side) I have my play partner write their name, (the name that is on their driver's license), address, date of birth, driver's license number, any type of medical conditions, medications, drug allergies, and the name and contact information of someone that knows that they are kinky. This person could be a significant other, brother, sister, co-worker, hair-dresser, babysitter, or housekeeper.

> "Sometimes I will not ask for a kinky contact if their partner is present at the dungeon where we are playing. I have an ICE card that contains all of my information. It is laminated and I keep it in my toybag. During the negotiations, I remove it and show my potential play partner that I have done the same. During our play session, our cards are placed face down on a small table adjacent to our play space. When our play session is over, each person will pick up their ICE Card and go on their merry way.

> "During negotiations, I explain that the information on the card is only going to be used in the

event that they are unconscious and the paramedics are called.

"This is the theory of the ICE card. Feel free to edit/ expand."

I like this idea and thank Sh3ph3rd for permitting me to include it in this book.

Safety and your toys

Tops are responsible for maintaining a safe environment for their play partners. Because sexually transmitted infections are carried through body fluid or blood exchange, clean toys are a key aspect of safe play.

While you can find more detailed toy-cleaning directives on the Internet, here are some general suggestions.

If you're cleaning anything containing batteries, remove them. Since you can't submerge electrical components in water, clean them with a damp, soapy washcloth—preferably with a commercial disinfectant. If you *do* manage to submerge something electrical in water *don't try to turn it on until you're sure it's dried out* (you might give it a few days).

You'll save yourself cleaning time if you start out by using condoms to cover all the sex implements that you can. And don't forget to have non- latex condoms available in case the recipient is allergic to latex.

Cleaning non-porous materials such as glass, stainless steel, hard plastic, and silicone:

- Glass: Wash glass implements with soap and water. Some glass products (such as Pyrex™) are not recommended for dishwashers. Do not expose non-Pyrex™ glass to extreme temperatures; it can shatter—explosively.
- Stainless steel: If attached to an electrical device, use

Toy handling tip

Place your scene toys on plastic (or a clean piece of cloth) when you set them out before play at a play party or dungeon. Don't place them directly on some table or bench—you don't know anything about the cleanliness of that surface. Clean toys risk becoming contaminated if you place them on a contaminated surface.

One time, as I was starting to set up my equipment for a guest presentation, a DM hurried over and (with a certain amount of disdain in his eyes and a sheet of plastic in his hands) explained that in their dungeon, plastic under toys to be used in a scene was a requirement, not a request. Point taken: I now put protection between my toys and any table/bench surface.

warm anti-bacterial soap and water (and don't submerge the electrical components). If there are no electrical components you have three options for stainless steel: Boil, or soak in a bleach-water solution (50:50 ratio) for 10 minutes, or wash it in the dishwasher and then use a disinfectant such as CaviCide™.

(CaviCide™ is a convenient, intermediate-level surface disinfectant that is effective against most viruses, bacteria, and fungi. <u>Products such as CaviCide™ are disinfectants, not cleansers—you must clean and dry an item before using the disinfectant</u>. If you're using a product such as this, it's not the wiping of the surface that kills the bad bugs; it's letting the chemicals dry on the surface for 15 minutes or so. When in doubt, follow the product directions.)

• Hard Plastic: Clean with soap and water or commercial disinfectant. Do not boil.

• Silicone: You can choose from three options to clean a silicone toy. Either boil it for 5-10 minutes, put it in your dishwasher on the top rack, or wash it with soap and warm water. Do not boil silicone vibrators, you will destroy the vibrator mechanism.

Cleaning porous materials such as rubber, vinyl, cyberskin, nylon, and leather:

- Rubber materials: Rubber materials are porous and difficult to clean. Worse, all rubber is not the same. You have no way of knowing the chemical composition of the rubber toy in your hand, and all rubber contains some amount of phthalates. (Phthalates belong to a family of chemical rubber softeners used in many sex implements.) Medical research has shown some evidence that phthalate interferes with sperm production and possibly infant genital development. That's scientific subtle- speak meaning *avoid this stuff*. As there is no reliable way to clean rubber implements, the easiest solution is to cover your rubber toys with condoms.

- Cyberskin and vinyl: Cyberskin is soft and porous and is often used for dildos. Wash cyberskin and vinyl insertables delicately with warm water only. Air-dry and dust with a small amount of cornstarch to keep them from getting sticky.

- Nylon: Nylon harnesses and such can be machine- or hand-washed with a mild soap.

- Leather: Wipe leather products with a damp, soapy cloth or with leather cleaner. *Do not soak leather*. After cleaning, restore your leather item by using a leather conditioner. Protect metal parts from tarnish by applying a coating of clear nail polish.

- The *cracker* on the end of a whip: Don't bother cleaning whip crackers. Most whips are designed to change crackers easily. Since the used cracker is filled with the bottom's personal fluids, just take it off and give it to them as a memento of the scene.

Emotional safety in play

While a great deal is written about physical safety in BDSM play, little has been written about emotional safety—either in BDSM play or in BDSM-based relationships. As common sense tells you

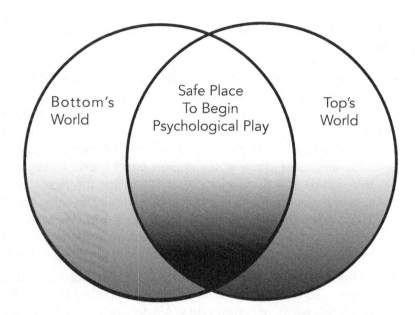

that you have to get to know someone a little before you invite them into your bedroom, common sense also tells you that you probably are going to need to know even more about them if you're intending to be their Top or bottom.

This little diagram depicts the shared area where both the Top and bottom know that they are alike and can safely interact. The more you share about yourself with your intended play partner, the greater is the common area where the two of you will feel that you can play safely.

This section of the book describes areas where your knowledge of your partner will help reduce the chances of emotional upset and increase the chances that you'll both have good play experiences. For a much more detailed discussion about *emotional safety* you'll have to go to our next book: *BDSM Mastery—Relationships: a guide for creating mindful relationships for Dominants and submissives.*

Emotional safewords

In the same way that you use *red* to signal that physical pain is too intense and the Top must stop, I promote the idea of creating emotional safewords within a relationship so the sub can signal the Dom when their feelings are hurt.

Since it is the protocol in BDSM-based power-imbalanced relationships for the sub to refer to the Dom as *Master* or *Sir* and not by his given name, I suggest that the two of you agree that if the sub calls the Dom by his given name, that's the signal that the Dom has hurt the sub's feelings and the two of you need to do something about it. Most commonly, I suggest you use *talking sticks* to work through emotional issues—but for that topic, I'll send you to another of my books: *Is THAT What They Meant: a book of practical communication insights.* That book is illed with communication strategies for D/s couples.

Upsets, landmines, and meltdowns

While I discuss *landmines* and *meltdowns* in Chapter 5 in the section on *psychological play*, I'd like to introduce the topic in the section on *safety. Landmines* vary in severity from "that's a touchy topic, please stop talking about it" to near-psychotic episodes. You won't often (if ever) encounter extreme examples.

Landmines are unknown emotional triggers that may suddenly get set off during play. Typically, they are unexpected and unpredictable and can be quite intensely violent. A Top can trigger a bad reaction through no fault of their own by recreating a situation that brings back a memory of a truly terrible experience. Depending upon the severity of the person's reaction, this may or may not be containable. If the person is not able to stop their reaction, you may have a total personal meltdown on your hands. This can be extremely serious and require professional help.

What they are:
- An upset: you've pissed them off.
- A landmine: you've triggered something from their past that has caused a reaction way out of proportion to the

present situation.

- A meltdown: the landmine was so large, the past trauma so substantial, that you may not be able to handle this one on your own.

How they'll look:

- An upset: they're fuming. They may or may not confront you about it right then. Some people go silent; others scream.
- A landmine: they, themselves, may realize that their behavior is out-of-control and are struggling not only to regain control, but they are trying to figure out what in the hell just happened. They're as shocked as you are.
- A meltdown: total loss of control. You may not be able to get near the person. They may be flailing and striking out or weeping uncontrollably. Total or near-total loss of personal psychological control.

Aftereffects:

- An upset: chances are—if you want a second date—you're going to have to apologize and figure out how not to do that again.
- A landmine: it depends whether the person knew of the triggering episode once it happened and was able to treat the episode as an unexpected reaction, or whether the episode opened up a series of memories that then triggered a series of more episodes over ensuing weeks or months.
- A meltdown: You may need help calming this person down, and the person may need psychological help in the coming weeks. Your follow-up will be critical.

Chapter 5
Negotiations and Play

In the beginning of this book, I said that I write in spirals: this is one of those spirals. I'd like to explain the interconnectedness of all this material in a slightly different way. Once you've decided to explore this *different world*...

- you first find a group of like-minded people;
- then you learn how to behave within that group;
- then you learn physical SM and mental D/s skills; and finally...
- you apply all you have learned to a relationship.

Over time, exposure to the BDSM culture (and particularly to SM play) will cause you to change your view of your own sexual and *relationship* wants and needs. After a few years immersed in this culture, you will much better understand who you are in the world and what you want from a partner.

This knowledge helps build a relationship with somebody that will meet your sexual needs and wants. **Connection is an important part** of any relationship and you will learn that intimate connection can be developed, strengthened, and reinforced through SM play.

Chapter 3 was about finding others; this chapter is about learning how to behave within our community. Chapter 5 addresses physical SM and Chapter 6 gives you some suggestions about bringing psychological power dynamics into play. But, for relationships, you'll have to go to our companion book, *BDSM Mastery—Relationships: a guide for creating mindful relationships for Dominants and submissives* (Book Two in the BDSM Mastery Series).

But wait! There's more...

This chapter is the first to introduce you to the *psychological* dynamics of our world. This is the point where we introduce the concept of *transcendent experiences*. In BDSM, a *transcendent experience* is one that is above average, special, spectacular. It is used to describe a scene where one or both of the players attained an altered mental state without drugs or alcohol. It describes the Top reaching Topspace (being *in the zone*) and the bottom reaching bottomspace (subspace).

As you learn more, you'll come to realize (as Guy Baldwin pointed out in *Ties that Bind*) that the path to *transcendent experiences* involves stressing the mind through power exchange (D/s) and stressing the body through SM practices. Whether you know it now or not, we're all in here to give or to receive transcendent experiences—peak experiences, experiences truly out of this world.

Negotiations and Negotiating

I've said it earlier but it's important, so I'll say it again: *Please start out playing with a new partner in a public play space. Don't agree to a private scene until you trust this person and feel comfortable with them.*

I know that this seems to be counterintuitive. You're thinking: "Gee—I want to get to know this person privately before I risk playing with them in *public.*"

Nope. Not a good idea. There is no supervision when you're playing privately. There is nobody to vouch for the Top should the bottom later claim that the play was non-consensual; there is nobody watching the bottom to ensure that the play is safe. You are *not* on a vanilla date; this is *not* just fucking.

Negotiation as a concept

Although the word *negotiation* makes this process sound formal and perhaps intimidating, *negotiation really just means agreeing upon what the bottom hopes to experience from the Top and what is okay and not okay for the Top to do to the bottom.* During discussions, you reach some understandings about issues such as physical and mental health, experience, and what each of you *intends* from your time together. The goal: to ensure that each person's *wants* are met without violating either person's *needs* (not to be traumatized or harmed physically or mentally, etc).

If you expect your scene to be successful, then your negotiations have to be successful.

Negotiation details

These discussions about negotiations are relevant for *pickup scenes* or for those new to BDSM scening. You won't be going through such elaborate negotiations once you've been part of the community for a while—unless you're playing with someone new to you. If you and your new partner have both been participating in BDSM clubs and parties for a few years and watched one another Top and bottom, the negotiations are more likely to sound like this:

Top: "Just to restate: I'll be using canes, floggers, and my hands for this impact play scene, is that right?"

bottom: "Yes, that's it."

Top: "And I can cane or flog your back, buttocks, stomach, chest, and thighs but not your pussy."

bottom: "Right: I'd prefer to save my pussy for a nice fucking session with you privately, if you don't mind."

Top: "Sounds wonderful. Is there anything I need to avoid—any strong preferences?"

Bottom: "Actually, yes, thanks for asking: I'm a bit claustrophobic, so I'd prefer that you not restrain me. Also, I don't need much warm-up, but watch my hands for my reactions. If all my fingers are stiff and pointed out, I'm processing pain. If my fist is clenched, I'm on the ride. I'll let you know if I need more processing time than you've given me."

Top: "Any landmines I need to know about?"

bottom: "Yes: please don't put your hands around my neck—it's creepy. And don't tickle me."

Top: "Okay, anything else about you that I need to know?"

bottom: "Nope, I've watched you play many times, and I love your style. Let's go."

In scene negotiations, the Top is asking questions to determine a few things:

- the bottom's physical and psychological interests and limitations;
- whether they can agree on the purpose/intent of the scene (to have fun, to practice a skill, to do power exchange...); and
- whether the bottom is someone the Top wishes to play with.

The bottom is participating in the Top's questions, of course, and (at the same time) asking questions and listening for certain additional information:

- whether the Top asks the kinds of questions that demonstrates that they have conducted scene negotiations a time or two;
- whether the Top appears to have the skills and experience to safely take the bottom on the ride of their life;

- whether there is the right *chemistry* between them for the scene to have a shot at being fun/enjoyable/successful.

While you can start negotiations by phone or e-mail, in-person negotiations are more effective because you need to be looking at a person to be able to read body language (to pick up non-verbal cues) and because the negotiation process, itself, is often used as the start of the scene—even if you won't be playing right away.

While the process of negotiating the scene may sound pretty boring and sterile, when done right it can be a lot of fun and very

---

Articulate or tongue-tied...

People differ. Duh. So... expect differences between how well the Top and bottom work through scene negotiations. Keep this in mind: a bottom is not necessarily a submissive. Top and bottom are position descriptions, not role descriptions. You can meet a rather shy but competent service Top and you will meet an aggressive, masochistic Dominant Top. So put your assumptions away when you're in our world. Watch how their personalities influence their play style. Learn.

There can be big differences between how well the Top and bottom manages the negotiation process. Some people are very articulate and are used to declaring what they want, and some people are more shy or timid about letting others know their needs. Both parties have responsibilities here. The Top must be careful not to overwhelm the bottom by bullying them into scene activities that would be uncomfortable, and the bottom must stand up for what they really wish the Top would do with them in the scene. I know that easier said than done

---

sensual. Use your imagination; try something like, "So girl, what's in that filthy little mind of yours?" and go from there. Remember, it isn't just the Top's responsibility to inject playfulness and energy into the negotiation and play; the bottom is also responsible for participating actively.

And, bottoms: You're responsible for the safety of your own body and mind. You're being dishonest if you tell a Top that you have no limits ("Anything you wish to do to me, Sir/Ma'am."). After all, you are not going to do something illegal or unethical just because the Top says it's part of the scene. You are responsible for getting your own needs met. Unless the Top knows your needs, chances are that they won't get met. The Top's needs may get met, but without clearly knowing *your* needs, the Top has no incentive to do anything more than he or she *wants to* do. This is not a great formula for success in the BDSM world. Many Tops, my partner included, simply won't consider playing with someone when they say that the Top can do anything that they want. Most Tops want their bottoms to know themselves better than that. Even if they don't think that the Top can hurt them, they need to be able to explain where *hurt* lives and what the Top needs to know to avoid that path.

Typical areas you'll want to cover during your discussions

Before I begin to discuss negotiation details, here is a list of topics that are usually covered:

- Logistics:
    - people involved and their roles;
    - time and place for the play scene;
    - how long you'll be playing (15 minutes or two hours); and
    - safewords.
- Limits:

- o what's okay to do;
- o what *might* be okay to do (your *maybe* skills/ sensations);
- o what is absolutely *not okay* to do (such as blood, scat, golden showers, etc.); and
- o intimacy level (touching, penetration, fluid exchange).
- Fine points:
    - o the intensity of play (marks, humiliation play);
    - o new or old injuries, physically or psychologically limiting issues (claustrophobia, etc.)
    - o emotional landmines (emotional or sexual abuse?)
    - o relationship status (as in, are you in one?) and do you have permission to play?
- Sex (penetration with or without SM, fingering…)
- Intoxicants/drugs
- Medical history, concerns, or issues
- Follow-up

Now, on to the details. Oh, you thought those *were* the details. Silly boy, silly girl…

A word about saying *yes* or *no*

For most of life's questions, a simple *yes* or *no* answer is close to useless. For example, the full answer to the question "Would you like to go out to dinner?" hinges not only upon who's asking, but what restaurants are being proposed versus meals that would be available at home, your energy level, your past experience going to dinner with this person and on and on and on.

As all executives know, if you ask poor questions, you'll get poor answers. When negotiating for activities that law enforcement officials are likely to consider illegal, it is in your best interest to learn how to be sure just how much consent you're getting when you, as the Top, ask the bottom whether they would like you to do X or Y to them.

Recently, my friend Rose (who owns the Austin BDSM club *Voyagers*, previously cited) described a method of calibrating yes/no answers in order to measure how *intensely* someone feels about that "yes" or "no." Rose pointed out that by asking a person to rate their "yes" or "no" on a 1-10 scale you will get a good idea of how emotionally connected they are to that "yes" or "no."

I like this idea a lot, and recommend it to you when you need to calibrate a *yes/no* answer on virtually any topic. This calibration system is particularly valuable when negotiating SM play. For example, if the bottom is giving you a *level 8 yes* to flogging but a *level 9 yes* to spanking, you'll know that you're good to go for both, but to lead off with the spanking. Similarly, a *level 6 yes* to flogging, gives you a lot of information about the intensity with which you should be flogging them.

Let me hasten to add that there are some subtleties involved with calibrating in this way. Not all actions carry the same emotional importance. For example, if YOU want to go to restaurant X at a *yes-10* level but your partner only is interested in that restaurant at a *yes- 4* level, whether or not you exert your will and go to that restaurant is largely irrelevant in your lives. On the other hand, if you (as a Top) really want to do X to your bottom at a *yes-10* level but their interest in having this done to them is anything below a *yes-8*, you had better be *very, very careful about how much X you do and with what intensity*.

Tops: this speaks not only to your communication/ listening skills, but also to your honor and integrity as expressed by your

Landmines

Words or situations that cause an unexpected and often emotionally intense reaction in someone that developed from prior (and often suppressed) traumatic experiences.

resulting actions; bottoms, you must be honest when giving your Top a calibrated reply.

Typical discussion (negotiation) strategies

You're the Top. Think of negotiation as foreplay. What do you want to get from this scene? What does your bottom want to get from this scene? Ask! This is a time to discuss obedience and surrender; this is the time to ask provocative questions.

Perhaps the first question is one of *intent*. Is this a *power exchange scene* where one of you is clearly the Dominant and the other is clearly the submissive, or is this a *sensation-only scene* between a Top and bottom?

Unlike a non-D/s Top/bottom scene (where you can pretty much say: "okay, bottom, the spanking bench is open; let's go!"), a power exchange D/s scene requires some staging and subtlety. In fact, the remainder of this book is meant to help guide you with the psychological dynamics of D/s play.

So, let's get started.

The first step is to figure out the *kind* of scene you're planning (discussed in more detail in Chapter 6). The *kind* of scene matters because D/s scenes usually begin and end with some form of ceremonial embrace and power exchange. *What you say and do* (and *how you say and do it*) during the opening moments of your scene influences the Top's success/failure to establish the bottom's pre-scene mental state. The bottom's pre-scene mental state, in turn, impacts the success or failure of the entire scene. Overall success or failure can be tangible: did the Top and bottom have a transcendent (extra special) experience or was it rather like another day at the office—not much? Asked differently, was the flogging a flogging, or was it a flogging? If it wasn't something to write in your Journal, you have room to grow.

Said differently, the Top must learn to take psychological control and express dominance during the opening moments of a scene through words and actions. Tops must develop their own styles, to be sure, but in a general sense what you say, how you say it, and how you direct the bottom all combine in a good scene to demonstrate *leadership* and *flair*. Tops: you may have to step out of your comfort zones.

Speaking to the Dom/mes for a minute: After you've completed the scene negotiations but before you start to play, you may wish to give the bottom some directive—ask the bottom to get something or do something for you, even if it's to find a piece of cloth to polish your shoes/boots. If you are not going to be playing for a few days, you can still give an assignment of some kind. It doesn't particularly matter **what** you instruct them to do. You can tell them to dress a certain way or tell them to bring something particular to the scene that night, even if it's only a box of facial tissues.

Anything that you can think of along these lines helps bring excitement and anticipation to the playing; it's a form of flirting as well as a way to demonstrate control.

Sir_Dragon_Z adds: "I have a collar just for scening. I do a ritual before we start and explain the importance of the collar and the role I expect the sub to follow. I explain My intentions, make her kiss the collar, and then start the scene. When the scene is over and cleaned up and she has been cared for, we do a similar ritual before removing the collar. I praise her and she again kisses the collar to show it respect, then I set her free."

Topics for the bottom to explore with the Top: So you're a bottom and you've found someone that seems really nice. You want to play with them, but you're still a little new to this and you're not sure what you're supposed to do or know. Well, *knowing that you don't know something* is a good place to be: it's called conscious incompetence. It means you're less likely to get hurt than if you go into this with blind trust. (Remember—I'm a cynical 70-year-old.)

Perhaps the threshold questions are: Who is this person and why do you want to play with them? To have sex? To get some SM experiences? How long has this Top been in the scene? Is this Top interested in the same or similar kinks that you are? Said differently, how experienced are they in the types of play you're seeking? For example, if you're asking the Top to do X, how do you know that they know much about it? They may have been in the scene a while, but X may not normally be their thing.

I'll share a personal story. I'd been in the scene for only about two years. My wife and I were on a trip to see my father. Our route enabled us to spend a weekend with a *very* senior gay couple we'd met a few months earlier at a weekend BDSM conference in Austin. The Dom was a published BDSM author and had been a presenter at the conference; we'd struck up a friendship. During our visit, the topic of *flogging* came up, and the Dom of the pair asked whether I'd ever been flogged. I said that I had not and he offered to flog me. No sooner were the words out of his mouth than his boy said, "You don't know how to flog!

"Oh yes I do," he replied.

Not a great confidence builder. As previously noted: Just because a person has been involved with the public BDSM scene for many years and is known to be competent in some forms of SM play doesn't mean that they are equally competent in *all* forms of SM play.

So beyond finding out some of the basics about the person who wants to Top you, what else can you find out? Have they held any positions in any local clubs? Are they known for anything particularly positive within the community? Do you have friends in common?

This is a little different from jumping into bed with someone who turns out not to know much about being a lover; some of our activities can harm you when misapplied by someone poorly prepared or trained.

PhoeixRed points out that most Tops have their own specialties and if you're looking for a particular kind of experience, it's good to ask the Top about it. If you're not comfortable asking the Top directly, ask a DM or others about that Top's skill in delivering the kind of experience you're seeking. Really, you can simply ask, "I want to experience X— can you recommend an experienced Top for me?" Negotiations can end really fast when the bottom wants to experience something on the Top's hard limit list. Not every Top will engage in every form of play.

Topics for the Top to explore with the bottom: So you're a Top and you want to play with this bottom. Sounds good; perhaps the bottom approached you. Still sounds good. But there can be risks, particularly if you're not too experienced. So, we're back to the questions I brought up a few paragraphs ago: Who is this bottom and why should you play with them? What makes you think that they aren't certifiably nuts? Do they come with references? Do you know anyone who knows them?

Well, you probably want to get some questions answered, so I've prepared a few for you, broken down into groups:

Experience level questions a Top can ask a bottom:

- How long have they been in the *public* BDSM scene (member of a club as opposed to playing on the Internet or privately)?
- What good and bad experiences have they had? What have they learned from these experiences?
- What are their most and least favorite toys? Why these?
- Do they prefer *stingy* or *thuddy* sensations?
- Do they prefer to play standing up (Saint Andrew's Cross) or lying down (massage table)? Why? Physical limitations?
- Do they have their own toys? What kind?
- Is it okay with them if you use your own toys?
- How do they communicate during sex or SM play? Do they scream? Thrash about? Get sassy/bratty? Squirt?

Play preference questions a Top can ask a bottom:

- Are they thinking of role-play, SM play, psychological play
- Is the kind of play that they're interested in also an area that *you're* interested in? (That is, will you be stretching your skills/ competency in order to play with this person (not a great idea?)

Questions about medical conditions a Top can ask a bottom:

- Just ask them: Is there anything about their medical condition that you'll need to know?
- Are they taking any meds that could affect their reactions?
- Do they agree to play without any illegal substances or alcohol in their system?
- Have they ever had seizures, any history of dizzy spells, fainting?
- How about their knees and back, might there be any positions that would be uncomfortable?
- If you're considering any kind of play that would restrict their movements (e.g., rope bondage, plastic-wrap mummification, etc.), do they have any concerns about claustrophobia? Is there any history of breathing difficulty, panic attacks, or asthma?

PhoenixRed adds: "If they reveal a medical condition, you have to ask if they carry any emergency meds and tell the bottom that they must instruct you (as the Top) how and when to use them. Conditions like arrhythmia, heart conditions, and asthma usually have emergency rescue medicines associated with them."

You'll want to ask about emotional/psychological issues, too. Have they had any particularly good or bad scenes and kinky relationships? Find out a bit about those. Ditto for their history of physical or sexual abuse—it can be awkward to ask, but you'll need to know about areas where you could possibly trip landmines. For example, I know one lady who will let you slap her breasts and genitals and back and ass—but not her face: her father used to slap her. I know another lady who will let you slap her face and body but warns that if you stick your finger or tongue in her belly button you'll never touch her again. I decided not to ask her how that one got started.

As long as you're discussing intimate topics, you might ask about their relationship with *pain*—physical pain, emotional pain, and/or spiritual pain. (By the way, the best book we've ever seen about *pain is: Sacred Pain* by Ariel Glucklich (Oxford University Press 2001). It's not a kink book.)

- Are they masochistic or are they curious about the sensations?
- Do they seek humiliation or do they wish to be treated with reverence?
- Are they *asking* to play with you or *agreeing* to play with you?
- Are they playing for *their* pleasure or *your* pleasure?
- What do they hope to get out of this experience?
- Oh, are any *words* off limits (e.g., bitch, cunt, fuck, whore, etc.)?

That last question brings us to the topic of *limits*. What are their scene limits—particularly if you're considering some psychological play, such as, humiliation, obedience, or verbal violation? How about physical limits such as the *degree* of intense sensations or whether or not you may leave marks?

Are some body parts off limits (e.g., breasts, genitals, etc.)? If female, how about vaginal fingering? What about ass-play? Are there any types of toys that are specifically *not to* be used? If you're intending on engaging in sexual acts, are you insisting on following safer sex practices?

You'll want to discuss how long the two of you intend to play. If you are at a play party, you'll want to know how they intend to get home. Remember: The Top has total responsibility for the scene and for *fixing* or *cleaning up* any aspect of the scene that goes wrong.

While most negotiations go swimmingly, some don't. This is a time for each of you to rely on your sixth sense. Did you feel each was being honest with the other, did you feel respected, did you feel the questions and answers were made with integrity. Did your potential partner have references; are they known within the community?

By this point, you should be good to go—so long as you are comfortable together. Enjoy!

Protecting against being hurt or hurting another

For starters, be smart about what you're doing. When scening, always give yourself an out. For example, leave a *safety link* in bondage settings—some way that you can quickly get the bottom out of position (I've already mentioned quick-release snaps). Regardless of where you are playing, the Top must never leave the bottom alone. I recall one particularly vivid scene in a Stephen King movie where the beautiful woman was handcuffed naked and spread-eagle on the bed, the phone out of reach, with her lover dead on the floor from a heart attack. Not a good situation. But, on the positive side, her screams caused a very large, vicious (well-trained) wolf to push its way in through the partly opened door of the (of course) totally remote high-mountain cabin...

Don't get drunk or high if you are playing alone. "What? Playing alone? As in, nobody else there? Why can't I drink or smoke and do some SM play if I'm alone?" Answer: Because in an altered state, you might think that something is a really good idea when it's actually a really bad idea, and you're not going to realize how really bad that idea was until it's too late to undo it. Ever read about the "Darwin Awards?" They are short stories about people who have removed themselves from the human gene pool because their good ideas weren't so hot. They make interesting reading, and I urge you to look them up on the Internet.

At any rate, if you're going to be playing alone, you'll not want to tie yourself up to the point that you can't reach your cell phone.

Chapter 5—Negotiations and Play

In reality, this means that you must be sure that the cell phone is secured to you in a way that you can always reach it. Oh, and be sure that the cell phone is fully charged. Of course, a fully charged cell phone within your reach will do you no good if you are experimenting with autoerotic asphyxiation. So that leads to the conclusion: don't play with autoerotic asphyxiation (again, refer to the Darwin Awards).

But you know all this, right? And you also know better than to play with relative strangers unless there are other people whom you know and trust around to help you should the scene go bad.

Female readers will want to avoid situations such as this: You have gone out to an upscale hotel for a singles meet-and-greet. There, you meet a really handsome man with an exotic accent—and you've got a *thing* for gorgeous men with exotic accents. He's a brilliant conversationalist and, evidently, a successful businessman. You really like him, you like his body; he likes you, he likes your body. He says he lives nearby, and if you would you like it, he would be glad to take you over to his place for drinks…

You are single and think that this sounds like a great idea! He offers to drive you to his nearby home (although he realizes you've clearly driven to this social event and he will now have to bring you back to your car). You accept, deciding that he looks and sounds safe—so you don't bother to go back to your car for your cell phone. You proceed to his house where he graciously offers you a drink and begins to show you his BDSM toys.

Well, now. This is an eye-opener for you have never even *seen* BDSM toys up-close. He shows you his spanking bench and Saint Andrew's Cross—like props from scary movies; you are titillated. After about an hour, he calls you a natural submissive and you ask him to explain that word. After a little more wine and talk, he asks you if you want to be his slave. Your head is reeling. BDSM? What's a submissive? Slave? You're a nurse—how do you get to *slave*?

This was how the woman who soon became my slave (for eight years) first discovered that there even WAS a BDSM scene out there. She went home and looked up *submissive* and proceeded to find the meeting times of local BDSM clubs. I happened to be the door monitor when she walked in to her very first-ever BDSM event.

She was extraordinarily lucky, for the man that picked her up and took her home was well-known and well-respected within our local community; he is a fine gentleman with unquestioned integrity. While I didn't know him well, we'd met at a couple of play parties and I liked him. He turned out to be a close friend of one of my close friends. Small world.

So, what else can you do to keep yourself safe? First and foremost, conduct your negotiations honestly and with integrity. After that, acquire skills. Then, practice those skills as your bottom practices using safewords during play. During this time, be careful not to play above your skill level and don't play if you've used any mind-altering substances before or during play. Last but not least, use safe-call procedures for new meetings.

Play parties for learning and practice

BDSM parties are places where people get together to socialize and do SM play. Some parties are *sex positive* (the politically correct way to say that fucking is permitted) and some are not. Some people dress up (leather, latex, vinyl/PVC, etc.) and some do not. Some parties require a specific dress code (to create a more coherent atmosphere and also to prevent voyeurs from taking part); some do not.

Certain standards of behavior have evolved to make play spaces safe and welcoming. If you'll follow these, you'll do fine

- If you see or hear something that offends you, quietly remove yourself from the area. If disgusted by a scene, PhoenixRed's approach is to say, "Oh, I think I'll go get a cookie." Leave that scene. Without drama, physically remove yourself from the situation and go somewhere else until whatever upset you is over. It is not the responsibility of those engaging in authorized consensual play to tailor their activities to someone's individual sense of propriety. Nobody has the RIGHT to cause drama because they don't like what they see or hear at a dungeon, demo, or workshop.

- Don't make assumptions. Don't assume that the men are dominant and the women are submissive. If a woman is wearing a collar, find out whom you must ask to speak with her; don't try to speak to her without permission—you'll be starting out on the wrong foot; people will talk about you.

- Don't touch anyone, their equipment, or belongings without permission.

- Respect everyone's privacy and discretion. Treat all information about party activities, attendees, etc., as confidential.

- Don't bring cell phones, cameras, or other recording devices to a party or dungeon—this can get you in a world of trouble. (Some conferences require you to sign an agreement that if you're caught with a cell phone in your hands, security will confiscate it for he duration of the conference.)

- Treat everyone with equal respect. Some people fill Dom/me roles; some people fill submissive roles; and some people fill staff roles. We're all just people trying to get through life and have a little fun.

- If you have negotiated a safeword other than *red*, please inform the chief DM or party host.

- Respect scenes. Limit conversation to the social area and screaming to the play area.

- Don't crowd the playing areas.

- Clean up after your scene. Use a drop cloth if anything may splatter the floor (ejaculate, candle wax, blood...).

- Don't play in the social areas or anywhere else outside the Dungeon Monitor's line of vision.

- Play sober. Do not bring alcohol or recreational drugs to the party (you may be banned). Smoke only in established smoking areas.

- Don't bring guns (even a toy gun).

- Obey Dungeon Monitors. They have the final word on everything including the right to stop a scene that they judge to be unsafe or abusive. They also have the right to tell you to leave the party or dungeon. (You're not going to want to talk back to a DM. Trust me on this one.)

- Be dressed *street legal* when arriving and leaving a party.

As BDSM interest has grown with the Internet, dungeons and private play parties have become more common and enabled more people to learn about BDSM. As newcomers began experimenting with SM play, they realized that some equipment is simply too big or expensive for apartments/houses. Many began attending BDSM parties in order to use Saint Andrew's Crosses, spanking benches, massage tables, and large wood or steel frames for suspension bondage.

Public dungeons differ a bit from parties in private homes because there aren't the same kinds of noise restrictions: the bottom can scream their lungs out in the way that really can't be done in an apartment complex or a neighborhood house without risking a concerned neighbor's call to the police. Public parties also offer exhibitionists and voyeurs socially acceptable places to play; what would be outrageous behavior outside the dungeon is perfectly normal inside the dungeon.

As you gain seniority within your community—and if you are well liked—you may begin to hear about *dark parties*. Dark parties are also called no-rules parties. They are just what they say they are: they are secret affairs that require a personal invitation. They tend not to use Dungeon Monitors. You may never hear about them unless you are part of a party-giver's inner circle.

While not everyone plays in public or plays with multiple partners, play parties provide outstanding opportunities for Tops to practice with a variety of partners and for bottoms to experience their own reactions to various forms of SM play by different Tops. In a general sense, everyone learns by watching the techniques

How to be a safe player

Negotiate the parameters of your play with others honestly and with integrity.

Acquire skills.

- Practice those skills.
- Use safewords during play.
- Be careful not to play above your skill level.
- Don't use any mind-altering substances before or during play.
- Use safe-call procedures for new meetings.

of others—which is why play parties at large conferences are often so full of people who are simply there to *watch*.

In a general way, there are three categories of public players: those who genuinely wish to play but can't do it in their own homes; those who use this as an opportunity to play with a new or established friend, and those that are practicing new techniques and are still a little awkward. Every so often you'll even find a Top who is really posturing for the audience rather than focusing purposefully (focusing with *intent*) on the reactions of the person with whom they are playing. One can only hope that this behavior will change as they grow in experience and self-confidence.

Some play parties may be gender-specific

When she reviewed this book, PhoenixRed wrote some comments to me about gender-specific play that I thought worth sharing. Although I revised her words to fit into my writing style, the ideas in the next two paragraphs are mostly hers.

When it comes to socials, hangouts, fellowship, demos, and educational seminars, inclusivity is great for such events benefit from people sharing diverse views and opinions. However, when it comes down to actually **doing** the kinds of things that get us off, it seems that the majority of the heterosexuals want to be with heterosexuals, the gay men want to be with the gay men, and the lesbians want to be with the lesbians. Among other things, it takes the guesswork and awkwardness out of trying to figure out who you can ask to do what with.

Sooner or later, you'll attend an event where the play areas are restricted to those with certain sexual orientations. I encourage you to respect those restrictions: don't go in there. The energy in gay, and lesbian play spaces often differs dramatically from the energy one feels in heterosexual play areas. Experience after experience teaches that most heterosexuals will leave a play space rather than watch some of the consensually aggressive play that can occur during gay or lesbian scenes. While everyone has the right to leave a scene, their leaving alters the energy of the room when they leave out of disgust or fear. There is an air of primal brutality about two men together that few heterosexuals have experienced. Often, it scares them, and that fright can produce an overtly negative reaction. This change from *fright* to *overtly negative reaction* occurs because people don't like to show in public that they're frightened, so they mask it with hostility that may well become vocal and be overheard. In a public space, that negativity detracts from the energy of those who are playing. Because conference producers know about this, they often provide separate play areas. If you're watching something that makes you uncomfortable or is revolting to you, just remove yourself from the situation without commenting. Go watch a scene that you *do* enjoy.

What are you likely to see at a play party?

Okay now for the nuts and bolts of what to expect upon walking in the door to your first play part . I'll start with the paperwork…

Waiver: You are 99% likely to be asked to show your ID and to sign a waiver that basically says, "Look, there's going to be nudity and kinky stuff here. By signing this form, you state that you know you'll see this and it's okay with you. If you, yourself,

> "Cages, spanking benches, sawhorses, bondage tables. Scene after scene. Throaty moans, high screams, whining, whimpering, and groaning. Jesus, Mary, and Joseph. All his cop instincts shouted for him to get his cuffs out and start arresting people."
>
> — *Cherise Sinclair*, Doms of Dark Haven 2: Western Nights

want to participate, you agree that you'll use safewords. In any case, if you want to go in and you agree to obey the Dungeon Monitor, then sign below."

By signing the form, you are agreeing that you're there to play, not to cause any trouble; by signing the form, you're also affirming that if you're in law enforcement or a reporter, you're not here in any official capacity. You're agreeing to be courteous to others and to clean up any mess you make during play.

Nudity: Expect lots of nudity and expect to see things you hadn't yet thought of. Expect people to be nicer and more open than you had anticipated. If you are brave enough to tell the host that this is your first event, they are likely to offer to provide someone to serve as your contact point for the evening.

Party Orientation: After you've had your ID checked for age-verification and signed the paperwork, you may find yourself invited to a brief orientation session. If you are new to this club, it is courteous to attend the orientation session even if you're senior in the BDSM community. Said differently, it's an act of arrogance NOT to sit through a club's orientation session if it's your first time at that club's function regardless of your BDSM seniority.

The orientation session is used to go over the house rules, including pointing out areas where you may and may not go, the types of activities that require a Dungeon Monitor's prior approval, areas where food is and is not permitted, and about play restrictions in public areas. This is also the time that you will be reminded of the policy against drugs and alcohol, told about smoking areas, whether or not loud screaming is okay, and about the party's default safeword (usually *red*. You will be reminded to clean up your play area, and told about using the cleaning supplies after your scene.

Dungeon Monitor: A Dungeon Monitor (sometimes referred to as a Dungeon Master or Dungeon Mistress or simply a DM) is a person charged with supervising a playspace (or dungeon) at BDSM events such as play parties and fetish clubs. Training and experience count, gender or BDSM role-identity doesn't count (you may know them as a Dominant, a submissive, or as a switch). Their authority is absolute while on duty. They can stop your scene; they can have you removed from the party.

If a DM orders a play scene to stop, it must be stopped immediately. Dungeon Monitors have significant experience and/ or explicit education in BDSM and safer sex practices, and often have been trained both in BDSM safety practices and first aid techniques. When I went through my DM training in Austin, there were specialized workshops devoted to emotional danger signals and for protocols for removing someone from a party against his or her will. As DMs tend to be senior members of the community, it's a bad idea to piss them off.

While DMs often wear a special vest, hat, or armband, there are no dress standards for DMs. Hint: If someone has a hand-held radio clipped to their outfit, is wearing an ear-bud, and is looking serious- as-shit at large play parties associated with weekend BDSM conferences, you can pretty well conclude that they are an on-duty member of the event's security/DM team regardless of how else they're dressed.

Dungeon Monitors are responsible for ensuring the physical integrity of the equipment as well as the physical security of the people using that equipment. The number of DMs present is usually based upon the number of play stations and an estimate of the number of people that will be playing. It's common to see a team of Dungeon Monitors led by an overall Chief Dungeon Monitor. At small private parties, the host often serves as DM.

As you become senior in the BDSM community, you also may be expected to serve.

Typical written/posted house rules

Rules such as these are likely to be posted or be part of the paperwork you signed before you were admitted to the play space.

- No alcohol, illicit drugs, or weapons are permitted anywhere related to the party.
- Cell phones must be turned off. (Because it's so easy to use them to take pictures, cell phones are often totally prohibited, even for checking the time.)
- No photography of any kind is allowed.
- Conversations are restricted to the social area; no play is permitted in the social area.
- The house safeword is *red*. Once *red* is called, play in that scene must stop immediately as a Dungeon Monitor assesses the situation. That scene may resume only upon the DM's approval. *Yellow* is a lesser safeword, but a safeword all the same. *If yellow* is called, the Top will check in with their bottom and may continue the scene unless additional help is required by DM's.
- A DM may stop the play at any time if they feel the bottom's or Top's safety is compromised. PRIOR to beginning play, please alert DMs of any health concerns they should watch and be prepared for. If you (as a couple) use a special safeword (such as "Mercy, Master") you MUST explain that to the DMs prior to play.
- Tops are *never* to leave their bottom unattended during play. Should you need to leave the room, ask the DM or another trusted person to watch over your play partner until you return. This does **not** mean that you can ask someone to watch over your bottom to go out for a smoke.
- Usually, if you have invited a guest, you are responsible for

monitoring that guest's behavior and that guest must leave before or with you.

Typical unwritten house rules

In addition to the posted house rules, there are also quite a few unwritten house rules that people are expected to know. I'm going to list quite a few of these because I think that they will help give you a feeling for the tone and temperament of play parties, particularly private parties held in someone's home.

Topics you're assumed to know:

- Before going to a BDSM party, find out whether you should bring something to eat; many parties are potluck affairs. It's not the end of your BDSM social career to come empty-handed, but you'll not be starting out with your best foot forward.

- Most parties have a dress code. Please ask your host about this before the event to avoid drawing inappropriate attention to yourself. (Raising my hand timidly, I'll have to admit that I misunderstood the dress-code hints of my very first party's hostess and my then-wife and I showed up in what might be politely described as wildly inappropriate high fetish while virtually everyone else was in jeans and T-shirts. People stared—with good reason.)

- Arrive at the party at the appointed time. Some party hosts are very specific about this, particularly if they live in residential neighborhoods. (I've run into house rules that said, essentially: "Don't arrive early or late: If you're early, we'll put you to work cleaning, organizing, and setting up for the party, and we won't let you in if you're late.")

- Pay attention to the way people prefer to be addressed. Some Dom/mes like being called Sir or Ma'am and it is common courtesy to follow their preferences in this respect—particularly if you wish to fit in with the group.

- Eat before you play: drink lots of water, particularly if you're the bottom. There should be plenty of food.

- Regardless of how senior you are, help clean up before you leave. Don't offer and then wait for instructions—just do it. Those 10 used plastic cups, you gather up and toss out, or the empty dip dish that you wash and leave in the drainer to dry at 3 a.m., or the ice bucket you refill mid-party just because you noticed it was empty will save the host a lot of work and mean more parties in the future. And you'll be noticed and appreciated; you can take that one to the bank.

- Don't mention party participants' names when speaking with someone who wasn't present at the party. Never place on the Internet any information that contains someone's name. Even mentioning a name in a letter is likely to be considered breach of etiquette. Even though you are sure that the person you are speaking about is unknown to the person you are writing to, do not mention any names, nicknames, or other details by which a person can be recognized. It's a small world. (One time, I helped someone put on some complicated piece of fetish wear at a conference on the East Coast, and when I returned to Austin from that weekend, a friend of mine on the West Coast e-mailed me that the person had really appreciated my assistance and that it had helped to calm him before he had to go on stage. To this day, I do not know whom I helped and was astonished that he knew someone in San Diego who would then write to me. Message: Your courtesy and discourtesy will be noticed. Anywhere in the U.S.)

- Do not touch people without asking permission. Don't put a friendly hand on someone's shoulder. In particular, do not interact with a submissive until you've established that you have permission to do so. If the submissive is clearly with someone, ask that someone whether you may speak with the submissive: if the submissive is alone, ask first whether they have permission to speak (at all) that night. From there, ask the submissive if you need permission to speak with her. Do **not** touch anyone who is not in a relationship with you—not even a little friendly touch on the arm during an approved conversation. You could trigger a scene, and not the good kind.

- Thank the hosts of the party when you leave and then call or send an e-mail the next day.

Niceties that will help ensure that you'll be invited back:

- Try not to act too clueless. We've all had to enter this world as newcomers, but those at the party are not likely to know whether you're a newcomer or simply someone they haven't met before who is visiting from another club.

- This is a world of *mindfuck*—where you can get surprised that what you *thought* was happening was *not* what was happening. Do not assume that attire signifies the position. Simply said, while wearing a submissive's collar may signify that they are a sub, it does not mean that they are a *bottom* any more than someone carrying a flogger is a Top. The sub may be serving as a Top for a scene; the person carrying the flogger may be in service to a Top who intends to use the flogger on *them* later in the evening. You may be seeing an aspect of *psychological play*—and part of a scene. When in doubt, ask someone who knows them.

- Be tolerant of things you didn't expect. There will be a variety of kinks and people filling all kinds of roles at the party. They all deserve the same courtesy that you would expect from them.

- Watching and learning are fine—and are often exactly the point, but there is a social norm in each group about the amount of *appropriate* astonishment to show to those around you. In particular, even if you are fascinated, try not to gawk and point noticeably at stuff you personally have not encountered before.

- If you wish to ask someone if they'd like to play, do so, but if they say no, respect their wishes in a courteous manner. "No" means "no," but "perhaps later" means that you get to ask them ONE more time later.

- Just because someone is a Dom/me or Master does not mean you have to obey them. Just because someone is a sub does not mean they have to obey *you*. Only your own personal partner owes you respect/deference beyond common, everyday courtesy.

- *Even if someone lets you hold their flogger, it is courteous to ask again before striking your own forearm or swinging it through the air at an imaginary target.*

- There are some private parties where sex is allowed and some parties where sex is not allowed. You have to ask. BDSM is not equated with sex for many people.

- If you are new to BDSM and have not yet participated in SM play, please know that you are welcome to watch. Watch the scenes and ask as many questions as you need to, people are usually eager to answer them. This is a good way of discovering activities that might interest you and which of the local Dom/mes are respected and play in a fashion that appeals to you. (Caution: If the scene is still going on, ask your questions quietly, and NOT to those actually participating in the scene. If you wish to ask a question to someone who participated in the scene, wait until they've finished aftercare and returned to the social area.)

- Enjoy yourself, that's why you're here.

Scene etiquette

Sometimes an inexperienced observer who is surprised by the kind of play they're seeing speaks up during (or right after) the scene to ask, "Will you show me how to do that?" and then are surprised or offended when the reply comes back something like, "Screw you very much, goodbye."

Remember, these people have just been in a scene. If it was an intense scene, they'll still in some degree of Topspace and subspace after the scene has ended. *It is a gross breach of courtesy to speak to those involved in a scene until everything has been cleaned up and put away and those involved in the scene are clearly socializing.*

In the same way that you can embarrass yourself in various ways when you go to visit an exotic foreign land, you can draw attention to your newness in the BDSM world by not knowing the cultural traditions that govern behavior at play parties. Here are some of the more important points to keep in mind.

- Some people consider the scene to start as soon as negotiations have begun. If you see a couple in intense discussions, please do not interrupt them.

- Others want to have their play scenes, too. If play furniture and play space are scarce, ask the host for an estimate of a reasonable amount of time to use them. In general, your scene should not exceed 30 or 40 minutes.

- Be quiet when observing a scene. Be polite, and don't talk or whisper. Yours could be the remark that ruins someone's wonderful scene.

- Leave space for the Top to move, swing a flogger, etc., during a scene. If the room is too crowded, stand against the far wall or leave the room. If the Top asks you to move, then move! If you get caught with a whip or flogger or other implement it's *your fault* and means that you were *waaayy* too close to the action. Don't get pissed; learn to keep your distance. (NOTE: At large play parties, DMs will often enforce scene perimeters.)

- Do not address comments or questions to the Top or the bottom while they are playing. Similarly, do not try to start a conversation with the partners while they are cuddling together after a scene. What looks to you like a lull in the action is not the moment to walk over and ask how long they have been doing this. (I had a scene interrupted like this one time during a lull: I asked the guy if I could answer the question after I finished making her climax. After the scene, I went back to him to ask if he had any more questions. He didn't.)

- You don't have the right to argue with the DM or determine the level of intensity that's acceptable in other people's scenes. If you are concerned that the Top is hurting his bottom, please report it to a Dungeon Monitor. Don't be surprised if the DM approves of the play.

- Remember that sometimes people play in such a way that you might think that something is wrong, but it just might be their style. Also, they may be seriously advanced players and playing on a different level than you've seen before.

- Do not join in scenes, even if it looks like a free-for-all: it may well be a carefully pre-arranged scene meant to appear casual. Or, it might be that the Top is subtly signaling to specific audience members. Join in only if the Top clearly beckons you in. If in doubt, ask someone around you what's going on—or check with a DM.

- If you see something that you don't like or you think is controversial, PLEASE tell the homeowner/host about it before you leave. *Do not tell anyone else*; do not gossip about it. Give the host a chance to solve the situation.

- Party rules vary with regard to play involving body fluids such as blood and bleeding, so you'll have to ask DM's. In some cases, rules prohibit any such play; others require play to stop until the Top tends to (and possibly covers) the bleeding areas. I once encountered a rule stating: "If you fail to tend properly to bleeding areas, you will be asked to stop playing entirely." Blood play is always acceptable *if you are in a designated medical play area.*

- Pick up your toys and clean play furniture and play areas when you're done. Most parties/events provide sanitizing sprays and paper towels for this purpose. If any bodily fluids were spilled accidentally, clean them up thoroughly.

After-play etiquette:

- Unless they belong to you (as in: you've loaned them to this Top for a scene), do not ever touch or get too close to the bottom during (or after) a scene. Bottoms depend upon their Tops to recover from a scene. The bottom's physical and emotional well-being is the Top's responsibility during and after scenes.

- Give people time to come down. If you need to ask a quiet question (such as, "Would you like me to get water or a blanket?") address the Top, not the bottom, and be as unobtrusive, succinct, and quiet as possible. As you'll read in a few pages, the Top may be in *Topspace* after a scene and you may get an unexpected reaction if you approach at an inappropriate time. Remember: It is the Top's responsibility to set up the play area. It's just not your problem if the Top has forgotten the water or a blanket.

P.S.: Most people like to be complimented on their scenes. If you like the way a particular Top or bottom played a scene, they'll probably be delighted if you tell them what appealed to you. But (as I have said repeatedly), wait until they are walking about and socializing again. Asking interesting how-to questions is a good way to make friends.

Chapter 6
Understanding SM Play Scenes

> Sometimes a cigar is a cigar, sometimes a cigar is a dildo, sometimes a cigar is part of a fire play scene. You have to understand context. This chapter is intended to help you sort through the many and complex aspects to sado-masochistic play scenes.

Types of play scenes

Physical play

When you think about BDSM and *playing*, chances are that you're mostly thinking about the physical aspects—flogging, spanking and so forth. Kinky play actually covers a wide range of activities and intensities. When you're starting out, light play can be compared to going out for a walk, medium play might be compared to a mile-long jog, and heavy play might be compared to a 10km race. The 10km race isn't beyond reach, it just takes some preparation and coaching.

In addition to skill competence, the success or failure of a physical SM scene depends upon successfully combining *intent, appropriate communication*, and *integrity*. That is:

- you have agreed upon your mutual wants/needs and intentions;
- you have agreed to use SSC play standards and safewords; and
- both of you can be trusted to keep your word.

A note about that last bullet: Personal integrity in BDSM play means that the Top won't introduce any play during the scene that was not previously discussed and agreed upon and that the bottom will honestly use safewords. Complaints from play partners in either of these areas can set your reputation on fire—a smoldering fire that can last for years.

D/s role-play

Role-play—fantasy play—is probably the best known and most common form of psychological play. It's the stuff of bodice-ripper fiction books. You can find great books and websites filled with ideas: Here, I'm just listing of some of the better-known forms to give you a sense of the breadth of activities covered by BDSM play.

Ageplay

- Ageplay: one person acts and/or treats another as if they were a different age.
- Adult baby: just as it sounds: the adult is behaving as a baby— often below the age of toilet training (and thus will be wearing diapers).
- Big/littles: an adult, usually (but not necessarily) female, who needs, craves, desires, and seeks a parental/young-child type relationship. This is NOT related to incest or taboo sex. Even though most have sex with their "parent," they don't generally engage in sex while in little/babygirl headspace. Daddy/babygirl and Mommy/babyboy are included under this category.

- Daddy/girl (and all its variants): often a protecting/nurturing structure, but every-so-often, the girl gets out of hand and has to be *reprimanded*. (This structure is utterly unrelated to the prior (and similar-sounding) category of *Daddy/babygirl*.)
- Daddy/daughter: this, in fact, could be taboo incest play.

Pet play

- Animal-play: where a player is treated like an animal or enjoys going into animal headspace (dog, cat, pony, etc). NOTE: There is a big distinction between a person playing the *role* of an animal versus taking on the *persona* of an animal. (In pony- play, for example, if you go up to someone playing the role of a pony and speak to them, they will speak back to you in English. On the other hand, if you go up to someone in pony headspace and speak to them, they a will most likely act like a pony and toss their head, whinny, and paw the ground.)

Authority-based play (coercion play)

- Master/slave: where a player is treated as the property of the Master/Mistress.
- Torturer/captive prisoner: where one player is a captor who abuses the other.
- Kidnapped fantasy: the submissive player is bound, gagged, and possibly teased before the sexual act.
- Authority figure: where a player takes on the role of an authority figure and may bully or humiliate their partner into sexual activity. Some bottoms will resist (to preserve their purity) while others will reluctantly submit (the decision being clearly out of their control).
- Gender-play: where one or more players take on roles of the opposite gender.
- Medical fantasies: involving doctors, nurses, and patients.
- Uniform fetish: one or both participants dress in some uniform while the dominant participant plays the ranking

officer (e.g., naughty schoolgirl and principal; military officer and escort; two military personnel having a tryst).

- Forced orgasm: the bound bottom is repeatedly forced to orgasm.

- Rape fantasy: (advanced play—always at the bottom's request) where one player feigns being coerced into an unwelcome sex act.

- Prison fetish: role-play using a prison scene. (Given that real life prisons are same-sex communities, this fetish lends itself to male-on-male or female-on-female activities and settings. Opposite-gender play is also possible between inmates and guards. Prison-play can be a form of uniform fetish.)

- And on and on and on… There is a whole world of coercion fetishes for you to discover as you explore the world of BDSM.

When you're starting out in this culture, physical SM play and role- play are the most common activities you're likely to see or recognize. However, there are some forms of play that are less often discussed— and more difficult to recognize. I'll touch briefly on *psychological play* and *energy play* so you'll know they exist.

Psychological play (power play)

While virtually all Dom/sub or Master/slave play has a psychological component, I'm using *psychological play* in the sense that the activity's focus is mental rather than physical. This kind of play involves playing with a person's mind rather than their physical body.

Psychological play is one of the most intense and misunderstood forms of BDSM edgeplay. Unless you're seeing a big interrogation or humiliation scene, psychological play is often difficult to observe in public dungeons. In fact, you may not even realize that a scene is going on: to you, there are just two people talking. But remember— this is not the world of WYSIWYG. Yes, sometimes the two people are just talking, but—sometimes—one of them is holding the other transfixed as they twist and play their emotions like a fine musician.

You'll get the same hateful look if you interrupt them as you would if you interrupted a flogging scene. Beware.

There are some fun sides to mental play and some dark sides. This area includes hypnotism, humiliation, and degradation as well as *mindfuck* scenes that can require long (and often devilishly subtle) buildups. Midori, an internationally renowned presenter and expert in psychological play, distinguishes between a bottom being humiliated in fairly harmless areas versus being humiliated in areas that hit core values. The former can be a lot of good fun, while the latter can be much more edgy and potentially psychologically harmful.

Psychological play also encompasses scary kidnap, interrogation, and rape scenes. While you may have heard about these, please remember that the "victim" requested the scene and a lot of people have gone to a lot of trouble to make it happen. These are all advanced forms of BDSM play, and while you are not likely to encounter them as you are just starting out, if you *do* find an offensive scene where you feel that someone is being physically or emotionally humiliated or degraded, just move on (and go get a cookie).

You'll also need to be aware that in the same way that physical masochists derive pleasure from receiving intense stimulation that most people would interpret as *pain*, many psychological masochists thrive on being embarrassed, humiliated, and/or degraded in ways that most people would interpret as hard-core abuse. I know it's hard to understand. Because it's not my kink, I also find it ha d to understand.

PhoenixRed adds that the excitement comes from pushing boundaries, sometimes WAY beyond someone's comfort zone. For some, this is the only kind of activity that really challenges them or puts them into that bottom/submissive headspace. For some, this is the only time they truly feel they are not at all in control—and they seek those times when they have totally surrendered control to another.

Even though I've already discussed *landmines*, I need to mention them again. Psychological play can expose trauma that can actually be worse for the person than landmines triggered by physical play (e.g., floggers). Something may come up during the play—some subject, setting, or action—that triggers emotional reactions that are disproportionate to the event. For example, although the Top and bottom may be used to *rough body play*, one night that same Top may strike that same bottom slightly differently or in a slightly different place or use slightly different banter and trigger an emotional reaction that causes the bottom to go out-of-control. Suddenly, the Top is watching a screaming, enraged, hysterically crying bottom and hasn't the faintest idea what just happened.

Remember that in psychological play, as in all forms of edgeplay, accidents can happen despite reasonable preplanning. It's important for you and your partner to work through the psychological debris if you ever become involved in a scene that triggers a landmine. You'll also want to warn future play partners of this potential landmine area in order not to have this happen again. Ultimately, you each will have to move on in your own lives without placing blame.

Energy play

Energy play is an advanced topic that is kept fairly well hidden, even within the BDSM community and is beyond the scope of this book. There is a small but dedicated group of kinky folk who use the energetic connection between people to augment SM play. This is the world of *cathartic release*, some Tantric practices, and Reiki-like energy work. You'll want some form of guide even to start you down this path, although I'm not qualified to point you in any particular direction.

The general gist of this approach is that since energy lies at the core of all matter and since the body is matter, one can think of the body as comprised of energy. Those following this school of thought go on to say that one's emotional energy resonates with one's life experiences, personal and professional relationships, and belief systems and becomes encoded in cell tissue. Neurobiologists (such as Candace Pert) have demonstrated that emotionally charged thoughts and experiences cause the body to manufacture different neuropeptides, chemicals triggered by emotions.

Quite a bit of work focuses on what is seen as a dance of electromagnetic energy between people in close contact that is controlled by one's mind. They believe that by guiding mental energy with intention— breath, gaze, gesture, and touch—one can learn to achieve emotional and harmonic resonance with another. Some believe that this practice has the potential to open up deeper parts of their personality and energy body. There can be some unexpected emotional effects— usually quite positive, but also quite unexpected.

Some within our BDSM community have learned to play with this energy field, and one national conference is devoted to lectures and discussions about this form of spiritual connection (Southwest Leather Fest in Phoenix, AZ each January).

Scene? As in a scene in a play? Oh, is that why it's called *play*?

I've already spent quite a bit of time discussing *negotiations*, but I'd like to be sure that you realize that negotiations can be spontaneous— at a party and just before the scene—or be drawn out over many days/ weeks. The longer negotiation period is common as you're getting to know one another or if the proposed scene is complex. (Mindfuck scenes, kidnap scenes, and other such complex scenes involve a lot of work. JLubeJack, who is a national presenter on mindfuck scenes, related a rape fantasy he directed one time that involved 11 people— including the local police— and took six months to set up.)

Often, the negotiation period actually starts the scene. The Dom/ me builds expectation, excitement, and possibly some fear so that the bottom is already in a heightened state of arousal by the time the physical aspects of play begin.

Scene structure

BDSM *scenes* are comprised of a number of discrete elements that I'll be covering in detail in the next chapter: *Anatomy of a Scene*. Now, I am only meaning to introduce you to the concept, these are the five key elements:

- the negotiation phase;
- pre-scene activities;
- activities during the scene;
- aftercare; and
- follow-up debriefing

By way of analogy, it's rather like taking a date out to a dance. You start by asking the person if they would like to go to the dance (negotiation stage), you get dressed, pick them up, and drive them there (pre-scene activities), you dance (the scene), you talk after the dance and have drinks together (aftercare), and you call back the next day to thank them for going to the dance with you (de-briefing).

Continuing the dance analogy for a moment: In the negotiation phase, you have to determine the particular *kind* of dance that you're offering (nightclub freestyle? country-western? swing? Latin? etc.) and *their level* of dance (e.g., social dancing, studio dancing, competitive dancing). The general message is this:

- If you want future dance dates, you'll want to take your partner to the kind of dance environment where they'll feel comfortable and you'll dance to your partner's skill level.
- If you want future BDSM dates, you'll want to verify that their wants are within both your and your partner's experience and skill levels. Your purpose is not to show off or be edgy; your purpose is to have fun so they'll do this again with you (why else is it called *play*?).

I'd like to mention some important concepts before I discuss common terms used in scenes and scening.

First, as Guy Baldwin pointed out in *Ties that Bind*, BDSM scenes are built around SM skills. SM skills, like skills of all kinds, improve with practice; skill acquisition is cumulative. Thus, the more you practice, the better you'll become with your SM skill—and the more satisfaction both of you will get from the experience.

Second, scenes tend to close the distance between people—they are intimate, authentic, unprotected, vulnerable, naked experiences. Be prepared for the emotional aspect of a scene.

Third, those who get involved with BDSM in the first place often do so to get a better understanding of how they fit in this world. Intense scenes change us in subtle and not-so-subtle ways.

Fourth, scenes last as long as they last. In a public dungeon, courtesy requires you to limit your play to about 30–45 minutes; private play can last from seconds to months.

So, on to some of the key components of scenes…

Subspace

Subspace refers to the psychological state caused when SM play triggers endorphins and adrenaline to be released throughout the body. While subspace can be elusive, it is most likely to occur when five conditions have been met:

- the players trust one another;
- the physical setting is conducive to that particular kind of scene;
- the psychological mood is right;
- the Top's SM skills are being applied to match the bottom's experience level; and
- their kinks match—players get sexually aroused/thrilled by this kind of play.

Because each of these five conditions contain so many uncontrollable variables, you can readily understand why many bottoms have never experienced subspace at all.

Subspace is a metaphor for the bottom's mental state during a deeply involved play scene. Many types of SM play invoke strong physical responses. Bottoms experiencing both the physical and psychological aspects of BDSM may mentally separate themselves from their environment as they process their experiences. They zone out. For this reason, deep subspace is often depicted as a trance state in which the bottom is submerged in a sea of emotions and is disconnected from their *thinking self*.

It's easy to understand that someone roused suddenly from a trance will be disoriented and incoherent. This is particularly likely

---

Some technical relationship notes about scenes and roles

While a slave or a submissive may consider themselves to be owned within the context of their relationships, the submissive usually retains enough personal power to call red to end a scene when playing outside of their power-imbalance relationship.

When it comes to BDSM play, a slave generally does not have the option to call red because their ongoing willingness to live in the Master/slave structure carries with it implied consent flowing from their pledge to serve and obey their Master.

If your purpose is primarily to get experiences or sensations and there is no submission, then you are said to be in a "Top/bottom scene" as opposed to a "D/s scene."

In a relationship, the submissive submits her will to the Dominant on an ongoing basis; in a scene, the person is only giving up personal control for the duration of the scene.

---

if something goes wrong in a scene and the bottom's arousal from subspace is sharp/dramatic/sudden. If the interrupting event is perceived as threatening, the bottom's brain may trigger their body to release even more adrenaline (on top of the endorphin/ adrenaline mix already coursing through their bloodstream). That can add a huge dose of fight-o -flight response to their disorientation and is an example of how a good scene can end in a heartbeat—often having long-lasting negative consequences.

Although most BDSM workshops and seminars focus on teaching physical skills such as bondage, impact play, fire play, etc., I have yet to see a workshop about how to be a good Top and a good bottom. That's surprising, actually, since a Top's ability to drop their partner into an altered mental state relies heavily on two factors: how well the Top can read their bottom's verbal and non-verbal signs, and how well the bottom can communicate their mental and physical states to the Top.

Correctly reading the bottom enables the Top to control how quickly or slowly the bottom will go into subspace, how long they remain in subspace, and how smoothly they come out of subspace—presuming that the bottom is in the mental state to go into subspace at all.

When reading a draft of this book, PhoenixRed commented that the Top is never guaranteed to be able to get someone into an altered mental state because it depends as much as anything on the bottom's state of mind when entering into a scene. A bad day on the job, the wrong kind of scene music playing, kids being particularly pesky, etc., can prevent someone from going into subspace.

Some people consider *flying* to be different from subspace. This is an advanced topic, so I'm not going to go into a lot of detail. Many who use BDSM for spiritual purposes have learned how to set up a spiritually-based play scene in which the bottom has out-of-body experiences. My former slave and I played this way a number of times.

We would begin by *cleansing the room* (a Native-American practice

Endorphins

Endorphins (endogenous opioid inhibitory neuropeptides, in case you wondered) are produced by the central nervous system and pituitary gland. The term implies a pharmacologica activity as opposed to a specific chemical formulation. The wor consists of two parts: endo- and -orphin; these are short forms of the words endogenous and morphine, intended to mean "a morphine-like substance originating from within the body."

involving words, gestures, and smoke from a smoldering sage-bundle) as Shamanic music was playing. We used Shamanic music of one kind or another throughout the scene. Typically, I'd take her under using what is called *Devil's Fire* or *cell popping* (a form of fire play wherein a red-hot dissecting needle is touched lightly to the surface of the bottom's skin at various places to induce an endorphin release). It was nearly instantaneous. Once her eyes rolled back and she was gone, I had to closely monitor how long I'd let her fly; the longer you permit the bottom to fly like this, the harder it is on their mind and body when you bring them back. When they come back, they'll be physically exhausted. It used to take my slave a good 30 minutes to be able to feel normal enough to walk. She always brought back stories of her astral travels. (My DVD/book titled: *Fire Play: A Safety Training Course* is available on Amazon; it demonstrates how to do Devil's Fire.)

There are some play implications of subspace. As a Top, your play will improve as you understand the interplay between emotional states and thinking states. For example, you can snap your bottom out of their beautiful, floaty experience by asking a thought-provoking question. It can be hard for someone to refocus quickly to recognize even that you're expecting an answer. If a scene is well underway and the Top asks the bottom a casual question, the Top will notice a few things:

- The bottom isn't too happy about having to leave their emotional state to return to their cerebral state to answer the question **unless it's safety-related**. (Thus, it's a bad idea for a Top to interrupt the flow of he scene to ask: "How are you doing?" As the Top, it's your job is to be able to read how the bottom is doing without asking.);

- The bottom may not be present enough to tell you that they are in an uncomfortable position, that a limb has gone numb, or that the sensations are too intense. (This is where your SM play safety-training becomes critical.)

About the term *subspace*

The term subspace began its life as the phrase, "the sub's space"—meaning the headspace that the submissive bottom enters once the SM play has caused endorphins and adrenaline to be released throughout their body. Over time, it was shortened to subspace. Its linguistic mate is Topspace.

While it is usually a submissive that is bottoming, that is not always the case. The bottom may be a masochistic Dominant (who may object to the term subspace).

Believe it or not, there is a surprise message in all this. As the scene progresses and the bottom is approaching subspace, their *reasoning ability* becomes impaired. There are two important rules to derive from this:

- first, is unethical to try to renegotiate during the scene; and

- second, the bottom can't be relied upon to use either verbal or physical safewords.

Message: If you want your safeword to work—particularly when your bottom is in subspace—you'll have to practice it.

Speaking of safewords and emergencies, if a bottom is heavily into subspace when an emergency occurs (or if someone obtrusively enters the scene uninvited), the Top needs to understand that they can't count on much help from that bottom. In fact, there is a risk that a bottom that is suddenly aroused out of deep subspace will act irrationally and actually add to the complexity of any emergency that the Top is trying to manage.

It is the Top's responsibility to remain aware of all of these things. It is an immense responsibility.

Topspace

As opposed to subspace—which is largely endorphin-driven—Topspace is largely adrenaline-driven. That means that while your bottom may be zoned out, you may be on high alert.

Although I have not heard of it being discussed previously in BDSM books, when a Top is in what we call Topspace, they are actually experiencing what psychologist Mihaly Csikszentmihalyi initially described in 1993 as Flow or Optimal Experience. His research led him to conclude that:

- when people are wholly involved with (and focused on) a task at which they are expert; and

- when they are getting real-time feedback that affirms that they are being successful; and

- when their concentration is so intense that there is no attention left over to think about anything irrelevant or to worry about mundane problems, then they enter a state where nothing else seems to matter. Self-consciousness disappears and their sense of time becomes distorted.

These experiences—immediately recognizable to experienced Tops— are so enjoyable that people will do them for the sheer sake of doing them, even at great personal cost.

Aftercare

I first want to talk about basic aftercare for the Top and bottom. A scene doesn't end when the toys are put away. *Aftercare* describes actions that enable the Top and bottom to regain personal control physically, emotionally, and mentally. As most Tops worry about actually hurting someone they care about, aftercare also serves as a time when the bottom can reassure the Top that the Top did what they (the bottom) had agreed to.

Let me go into this in some detail, as *aftercare* is as important for most scenes as an ending is for a story.

Aftercare is the most obvious and practical way to help combat emotional drop at the end of an intense scene. It's important that aftercare lasts long enough for the bottom to be able stand up and walk around and for the Top to feel the adrenaline drain out of their system.

Aftercare is a time to acknowledge (worship, if you will) the gift that the other has given; this is a time to pay tribute to their body for what they just *took* or went through; this is a time to complete you bond with this person. And, during aftercare, you should touch every part of their body, not just where you were playing.

Aftercare is a way of letting the bottom know that they're in a safe place and for letting the Top know that they did a good job. Perhaps the best thing a Top can say to a bottom after a scene is, "Thank you, you were a good bottom and I enjoyed playing with you." Perhaps the best thing that a bottom can say to a Top is: "Thank you for giving me those sensations. You did a good job. I feel fine, now, and my head is starting to stop spinning! I hope we can play again, sometime."

Now, even if you knew that, here is a bit more: this will make increasing sense as you gain experience in play scenes. Aftercare, as was pointed out to me recently by my friend Master Shack from San Antonio, is a form of *exduction* from an hypnotic trance state. Exduction is the opposite of *induction*. During aftercare, you have the perfect opportunity to return the bottom to *normal headspace* filled with positive thoughts and feelings. During aftercare, you can say such things as: "You're feeling well. You're feeling good; you've had a wonderful experience." This is a time to get them to focus on *themselves*.

Now, there are some issues that complicate basic aftercare. Aftercare is as important for the Top as for the bottom. But that doesn't mean that this is always a warm, fuzzy, and cuddly time. If the scene has involved particularly heavy play, a Top may not be psychologically able to switch gears on a dime in order to be cuddly for their bottom. Similarly, (as PhoenixRed commented to me) the bottom may only need to be asked if they're okay. Often, they don't want cuddles, they want privacy as they're putting themselves back together psychologically. Not all subspace is floaty and joyful; sometimes they're dark—but not a bad *dark*. Similar to *good pain* and *bad pain*, there are good dark places and bad dark places a bottom can go during a scene. It's up to each person to get their own needs met and to safeguard their own physical, psychological, and emotional safety.

Along an entirely different track, in big play parties, the Top is responsible for immediately cleaning up the area to enable others to play and the DM simply won't permit time for cuddly aftercare. Because we all know that, if a Top knows that the bottom will need an emotional cool-down period, they may ask a mutual friend to provide aftercare for a few minutes. This is far from ideal, but it is better than the Top largely ignoring the bottom to clean up the play area as the bottom is struggling to regain emotional and mental balance.

More aftercare subtleties: There may be specific and valid reasons why the Top does not want to be the person providing the aftercare. For example:

- The Top may be playing with someone else's partner or property.
- They are not intending to build a relationship.
- The Top may be demonstrating SM skills with someone

they don't know and don't particularly want to know.

- The Top may know the bottom and specifically NOT want to bond with them for personal reasons.

In these cases, it's a good idea to find another person (called a *third*) who understands the reasons that the Top does not personally want to perform the aftercare and agrees to observe the entire scene and be responsible for the bottom's aftercare at the end of the scene.

Post-scene realities

One hears much more about the excitement and mystery of subspace (and even Topspace) than about the aftermath. Both Tops and bottoms often have to cope with the realities of life after scening. Top-drop and sub-drop refer to the wave of reality that washes over people who have become emotionally drained during an intense scene.

People react differently after heavy or intense play. Most people are reasonably well recovered within 20–40 minutes, but some bottoms get a bit depressed, want to be left alone, or want to sleep it off. As people react differently to SM scenes, your best policy is not to build your own ideas of "right" or "wrong" aftercare on the scenes of other people. Learn to read your own play partner.

Top-drop can be particularly harsh when the Top has to come back to reality and ensure that the play space is cleaned up and that the toys are put away. Often, the Top has to pull away from the bottom that they *know* needs emotional care. This sharp change from Topspace to managing scene logistics (while largely ignoring their partner) can be extremely uncomfortable.

Aftercare is the antidote for sub- or Top-drop.

Cleaning up: When you're playing at a play party, you are responsible for cleaning the space for the next players. Whether the Top or the bottom cleans the area depends both upon their particular

Not all scenes end with aftercare

While this note applies to advanced players, you should know about it, lest you draw some inappropriate conclusions in the dungeon.

Aftercare is not appropriate for all scenes. For example, some mindfuck or punishment scenes depend on the bottom processing the experience on their own: a cuddling-type of aftercare would negate the intent of the scene. Similarly, when a true sadist is playing with a true masochist, cuddly aftercare is the opposite of the way the sadistic Dom/me would end the scene.

dynamic and upon the kind of scene they just had. PhoenixRed has mentioned that especially in D/s and M/s relationships, if the sub is physically and mentally okay, the sub is likely to be directed to help clean up the space or to clean it up totally on their own. Actually, some D-types use the scene cleanup process to help restore their sub/bottom to normal cognitive functioning. That is, they use the cleaning process, itself, as a ritual upon which the sub can focus after a scene. Also, *packing up the toys* gives them a quiet time to reflect on the scene they just had. After the scene, the sub usually goes right back into service mode. Of course, the D-type will monitor them during this post-scene clean-up and help out (or completely take over) if need be.

Closing the scene–notes for Tops: It's not quite appropriate to end a scene and say goodnight to your partner and just leave it at that. You've just shared intimate experiences. For the sake of your reputation—to say nothing about getting a chance to play with this person again— call them a day or so after the scene. This is the last act of your play: the debriefing

Unless you live with them, it is simply common courtesy to call your scene partner a few days later to thank them again for permitting you to play with them and to be sure that they are physically and emotionally okay. I strongly urge you to speak together on the phone rather than by e-mail; e-mails are too impersonal. Among other things, the bottom's inclination to play with you again depends upon how you handle the relationship after you each have gone home. Please don't skip this step or the person may end up feeling used (*Find 'em, fuck 'em, forget 'em.*).

But, there is more to it than that.

Contacting your play partner a few days after the scene enables the Top to learn first hand about anything that might leave the bottom with a negative feeling from what the Top did during the scene. As a Top, you're going to want to hear about an upset play partner from that person, not from someone else in the community who heard it from X who heard it from Y who heard it from Z. In this light, debriefing your bottom a few days after your scene is for your own good. It helps build your reputation as a trustworthy and compassionate Top.

The flip side of this lesson is that the Top who mishandles a scene and doesn't clean it up through aftercare and debriefing may find that their reputation has been tainted. While rare, I know of a few cases where a Top's bad scene behavior resulted in their being warned or banned from future play parties and, in the extreme, being shunned by an entire community.

Sir_Dragon_Z comments: "I ask the bottom to e-mail me about how the scene developed 2–3 days later, after she has processed her emotions and feelings. Then, after I've read it 2–3 times I call her to go over every comment— good or bad."

I'd like to add that I think that this is a fabulous idea, and I now recommend it whenever I'm teaching people about bringing closure to scenes—particularly when the bottom is fairly new to BDSM.

How a scene can go wrong (and what you can do about it)

It is really quite straightforward: scenes can go wrong in one of four ways...

- skills failure;
- accident;
- negligence; or
- psychological landmine.

If the scene went wrong because you didn't know some aspect of a skill that you thought you knew (or didn't realize was necessary to know), you now know what you need to study/learn. You now know that whatever skill you were using is more complicated than you thought: you now have the opportunity to learn and to grow. Apologize to the bottom (and to anyone else you feel may need an apology) and move on with your life.

If the scene went wrong because there was an accident, figure out what happened so you can avoid those circumstances in the future. But some accidents are harder to deconstruct than others, particularly in SM play, so you may need to ask some more experienced SM players to help you to understand the *critical failure points* (as they're called in production planning). Now, I'll go one step further. In fire play—my specialty—I've had two *oops* experiences and one time watched my co-Top have a more serious *oh-shit* moment. Each time this has happened, I carefully wrote out the experience and posted it to our club's eGroup and incorporated those lessons into my fire play workshops. It's about attitude; if you've had an accident, others are likely to have a very similar accident. You are ethically obligated to use your accident as an opportunity to teach or warn others about it.

If the scene went wrong due to negligence, was it *your* negligence or the negligence of others? If *you* were negligent, you have some soul-searching to do and you may very well need to make amends to someone—or a number of someones. This is a learning experience tied to your ethics. How you handle an SM play error of your own making will tell the community quite a bit about your own morals/ethics. If the scene went wrong due to someone else's negligence, then you have one very serious discussion ahead of you. If you are not used to having honest and serious discussions, I'd suggest you immediately purchase one or both of these books: *Crucial Conversations* or *Crucial Confrontations* by Patterson, Grenny, McMillan, and Switzler.

Cycling back to the *landmine* issue for a moment… if the scene starts to go wrong because you hit a psychological landmine, you need to know what to do.

As I've already said, sometimes something that a Top may do can inadvertently trigger a landmine. It's not that the Top did something that would upset another person, it's that the Top accidentally did something to trigger a flashback that is unique to that person. Most often, the root cause lies deep in the bottom's psychological past.

As you (the Top) start to sense the bottom's loss of emotional control, physical contact is often the best step: throw your arms around the person and reassure them that they are okay and apologize for anything that you did that might have triggered their response. The thing of it is, when it comes to landmines, doing X often produces result *elephant* rather than result *Y*, so it may not be at all clear to you as a Top what you did to produce "elephant"—thus it may not be clear what to apologize for.

If holding the person doesn't work, you can try bringing the bottom back to reality by giving them power. Ask, "What, exactly, do you want me to do right now?" You should speak forcefully but in a low and controlled voice. It's **very important** that you seem calm and in control. Your frame of mind should be that you're simply instructing the bottom to come present and help to solve this problem. Asking a question forcefully engages their mind and should help to pull them out of their emotional state. You should be firm, but if you are aggressive or overbearing, the situation is very likely to get much worse right away.

Now, if *that* doesn't work, you may have more on your hands than you realize.

PhoenixRed adds: If the landmine relates to a past abusive relationship where the partner was overly authoritative and then abusive in some way, using a forceful voice may make it worse. They associate that string of behaviors with bad things happening. The big thing is not to panic. Keep control of yourself even if the bottom seems to be going out of control. Be consoling and understanding and avoid getting involved with your bottom's emotions. Try to be the stabilizing influence they can latch on to.

Do not be overly apologetic, especially if the bottom did not tell you about this general psychological area during scene negotiations. You could say, "I'm sorry this happened," but you should not accept responsibility for someone else's psychological issues if you didn't do anything wrong. Just try and help them work through it and recommend professional counseling. Unless you, yourself, are a licensed therapist, leave this one for the professionals.

Now, here's a twist: what if you don't yet know how to evaluate a scene?

- *You think that the bottom is in distress, but you're wrong!* The loud sound of a bullwhip exploded in the public dungeon during one of my first DM experiences. This HUGE guy was using a 10' bullwhip on a petite girl who was screaming her lungs out. With some alarm, I started to move closer to the play only to be stopped by a woman leaning against a column watching the action. Seeing where I was heading, she very calmly said: "If you interrupt Beverly's scene, she'll kill you." Ooookkkaaayyy, then. Asking a few questions, I discovered that the Top was a bullwhip master and the bottom was a Harley- riding karate black belt with a passion for being bullwhipped. Who knew?

- *You think the Top isn't competent.* If you're watching an elaborate suspension bondage scene and it seems as though the rigger is losing control of his bottom, you won't want to interrupt unless you, yourself, know a lot about suspension bondage and believe that you see something that the rigger doesn't see. Surprises can be unpleasant, and you're going to feel like two cents waiting for change if you interrupt the scene only to discover that the guy doing the ropework is a national presenter on suspension bondage and knows perfectly well what he's doing. (I was there and boy, was he livid! He shut the scene down and he and his bottom left the play area.)

Scene trauma: (This is a cautionary note for newer Tops.) Occasionally, you'll hear of an inexperienced Top who began an SM scene and then abruptly stopped because:

- they realized that they weren't sure what to do next and were afraid of playing beyond their skill level;
- they became self-conscious with all the people watching;
- they realized that the person they had **really** wanted to play with is now available;
- the bottom did something to set them off (bratty remark, perhaps); or
- they didn't know how to slow the scene down to end it appropriately.

Whatever the reason, abruptly stopping a scene can leave the abandoned sub in a very *down* (and possibly publicly embarrassing) state. At best, they have to come out of "scene head-space" to take care of their weak/unprepared Top; at worst being abandoned by their Top floods them with pent-up feelings of inadequacy, self-doubt, and social mortification. (Just think of it: the person in whom they had placed their trust and body is publicly exhibiting poor self-control or poor ethical behavior. In our world, this type of person is called a *poor-quality Dom/me*. If seen publicly, this can have a lasting effect on one's reputation.)

This brings up a slightly different topic—the topic of a newcomer permitting another newcomer to play with them. If you are an inexperienced bottom and you permit an inexperienced Top to play you, you're asking for trouble. Not only are they unlikely to know how to read your body's reactions to their actions, they may not yet have a lot of precision with whatever toy/tool they are using, whether it is their hand or a whip. This situation creates a greater-than-average risk that the bottom will come away from that experience with bad feelings about it. If the new bottom has been physically or psychologically hurt in the scene, they may well conclude that, "If *that's* what BDSM is all about, I don't want any part of it" and leave our community.

Here are some lessons for you to consider:

- Bottoms should think carefully about the consequences of permitting themselves to be played by inexperienced Tops.

- Bottoms are advised to play with Tops whose prior play partners say good things about them.

- Inexperienced Tops should seek out experienced bottoms that are willing and able to coach them through *scene construction*. (Scene construction: Not only coaching about negotiating and using symbols before the physical aspect of the scene begins, but also coaching about how to build—and later reduce—the scene's intensity.)

- Being new to the scene doesn't mean someone is inherently dangerous—it just means that they're just not as good at these things as those with more experience. New BDSM couples who are uncomfortable playing with (or being played by) others can certainly practice and work on their skills within their own relationships. In a general way, new couples are usually encouraged to ask a lot of questions, get mentoring, etc. Nothing in this book or in the BDSM community suggests someone in a committed monogamous relationship has to play with an experienced Top or bottom instead of their own partner if that breaks a boundary in their relationship. Everyone has to find his or her own comfort level

Remember: Not everything in BDSM is as it seems. If a scene is making you uncomfortable, ask a DM about it. If the DM says that the scene seems to be okay, then go get a cookie.

Ultimately, it helps to know yourself as well as your play partner before engaging in any scene.

Chapter 7
Anatomy of a Scene

This section analyzes elements of a scene and explains how they can work together to produce an extraordinary experience. Whether you are new to BDSM scening or have been doing it for years, this portion of the book is designed to explain how to use elements of *psychological control* to augment the *physical aspects* of a scene. Overall, the intent of this section is to help you to understand how to develop a *defined repeatable process* in order to have *transcendent experiences* with your play partners (a *transcendent* experience is one that goes beyond the limits of an ordinary experience).

While some people live in a negotiated power exchange structure, when you are starting out in this culture, *power exchange* is generally seen as a temporary state. Two people get together as equals and agree to have a BDSM scene within defined boundaries. In that context, the submissive surrenders power to the Dom/me for the duration of the scene. The scene occurs and afterwards the dominant returns the submissive's power. Two people of equal psychological power go on to have a lovely evening. In this sense, power exchange is seen to have a beginning, middle, and an end.

As you gain experience, you'll realize that it's up to you to branch out from the general ideas in this book and use them to create scenes that fit *who you are* as a person playing with someone as a Top or bottom.

****

Because I'm mostly discussing *activities* in this book, I've been using the terms *Top* and *bottom* when describing scenes. You may recall that I'd mentioned that Top/bottom describe *actions* and Dom/sub (or Master/slave, Owner/property, etc.) describe *relationship roles*. I'm now going to describe a scene and include some psychological dynamics that involve Dom/sub behaviors and Dom/sub-speak. Again, for the sake of keeping sentences in this section free from "he/she" and "Dom/me/sub" constructions, there are going to be times when I'm going to write from the perspective of a male Dom and female sub even though, in reality, dominant and submissive roles fit people of either gender.

Now, I realize that I have gone over much of this material elsewhere in this book, but this is the first time that I have been able to bring all the concepts together in one place to demonstrate how they all flow together, so please excuse the redundancy. Also, I'm writing this scene out with a lot of detail

---

Why do a pre-scene scene?

A pre-scene exchange helps get the submissive out of their thinking state and into their *emotional state*. At this point, anything that you do that causes them to *think* rather than to *react* or *comply with a direct command* works *against* your purpose.

---

because it may help you better understanding about how various aspects of BDSM fit together to create a scene.

Oh—if you're fairly new to BDSM, you may want to stop here for a few minutes and do an Internet search for *Master/slave protocols* or *Gorean protocols* before starting this section. This section assumes that the Dom/me knows how to conduct a little on-the-spot protocol training for a new submissive bottom. (NOTE: The **Gorean** philosophy of a male-dominated Master/slave world sprung from John Norman's science fiction novels. There are both similarities and differences between the ways Master/slave relationships are enacted in the Leather culture, the general BDSM culture, and in the Gorean culture. There is substantial conceptual crossover.)

ajor note to Tops about scene collars

ɔ not EVER suggest that a collared submissive remove their gular collar OR put on your temporary collar along with their gular collar. You'll be showing your outrageous ignorance at e same time that you're deeply offending the sub and (quite ely) pissing off their Dom/me—who was nice enough to give ›u permission to play in the first place.

Starting the scene with a ceremony

Power exchange can be used to supercharge the connection during an SM scene. To do so, the Dominant can use a trick. Unless the Dom/ me is fairly experienced in BDSM and also experienced in psychology or Neuro-Linguistic Programming (NLP), they probably don't consciously realize what they're doing, or that it's something of a trick. The trick is to put the bottom—in this case, probably a submissive—into a nearly instant light trance state. There are a number of elements that a Dom/me can string together to trigger a light trance: the components include *what you say*, *how you say it*, and *how you touch them*. In this case, *touch* can include placing something symbolic on them, such as a scene collar.

Frame of mind: The Dom/me's key role is to trigger in the bottom what is called a state change in NLP. In this particular case, the task is to change them as quickly as possible from a thinking state to an emotional state. The easiest way to do this is to demonstrably take charge. This does not mean to be domineering or pushy, but it does mean to be firm, focused, and purposeful. The Dom/me can use anything that they can think of to get their submissive to recognize their authority over the impending scene. If the sub is uncollared, you may wish to put them in a scene collar. If the submissive is already your collared property, consider adding another symbol—something used specifically when you're having a scene.

Ceremony is good: Ceremonies anchor emotional memories. Good ceremonies anchor good emotional memories. The more you support and encourage (anchor) good emotional memories, the more automatically the person drops into the good emotional state the next time you begin the ceremony. It is basic behavioral conditioning: it's Pavlovian. (*Pavlovian* refers to the work of Russian psychologist Ivan Pavlov who developed the concept of the conditioned reflex. In his classic experiment, he trained a hungry dog to salivate at the sound of a bell by conditioning the dog to associate the sound of the bell with the sight of food.)

That's why conducting a ceremony before a scene is really part of the scene—you're already starting to affect the submissive bottom's expectations about the positive experiences they're about to have with you. D/s *protocols* are your path through this ceremony.

NOTE 1: You may not be able to induce a trance state with a Dominant bottom: they may not be able to relinquish enough control to get into the right headspace.

NOTE 2: For the remainder of this section, I'm going to refer to a male Dom and a female submissive. I'm doing this to increase the impact of the words.

So for starters, you, as the Dom, might want to consider doing what is called a *pattern interrupt*. You want to do something that is unusual to derail her thinking state. You can make stuff up if you have to—ring a bell, tear up a piece of paper. Almost anything odd/ unusual will disrupt her mind. Put her in cuffs; blindfold her. Require her to kneel, strip, and stand perfectly still for 18 seconds. Or, have her kiss your boots. Be creative. (There is a lot of theory supporting brain-scrambling techniques such as these for training. When my children were very young, I used to tell them that they had, for example, 22 minutes to clean their rooms. The time period isn't the issue; the *unusual* time period is the issue.)

Personal integrity in BDSM play means that the Top won't introduce any play during the scene that was not previously discussed and agreed upon.

Have some kind of prepared speech to give her. Hold her to you in some unusual, ceremonial way. For example, you can bring her right hand around behind her back and hold it with your right hand while you grab a chunk of hair just above the nape of her neck with your left hand. Don't yank on her hair, just run your fingers through it to get a good grip and *tighten your grip*. Now *say something that demonstrates your command of the setting*.

Reinforce how important it is for *you* to be playing with her as a person; make her feel extra special. Once on the equipment, touch her with authority, express control, pull her hair.

Sample opening ritual:

"tina, before we begin, I want you to remember that if you need some time to process the intense sensations you are about to experience, you are to use the safeword *yellow* and that if the sensations become too much for you and you want me to stop, I am instructing you to use the safeword 'red.' Do you understand and agree?"

(NOTE: These statements establish the Top's knowledge,

Major note

BDSM scenes are intense affairs. If this is to be a D/s scene (a scene involving psychological tension between a Dominant and their submissive), the sub should feel very grounded and bonded with their Dom/me when the scene ends. After all, that bonding is a key reason for playing in the first place.

However, if you (as the Dom/me) are playing with a submissive with whom you specifically do not wish to form a strong emotional connection, then I strongly advise you to have pre-negotiated that a trusted friend of the bottom will be available to do the aftercare so the bottom does not bond with you. I have ample experience of the entanglements one can get into before figuring this out.

authority, responsibility, and trustworthiness; these are important words to use to establish the serious tone that the Dom/me needs before continuing with the next series of phrases. This wording also helps to give the bottom permission to "red out" of a scene without feeling guilty.)

If she merely says, "Yes," then the Dom may use a dominance- reinforcing phrase such as: "tina, that would be, 'Yes, Sir,' " to which she then replies (meekly?), "Yes, Sir." At this point, the Dom may or may not give her a little hug and say, "Good girl." (Issue: You don't want to sound either condescending or patronizing or you risk breaking the mood as the sub suddenly thinks: "What an asshole to speak to me as though I'm a child!")

The Dom may then continue something like this: "tina, I'm now going to be in charge of you and use your body as I see fit.* You are now under my authority and control. Do you understand and agree?"

(* NOTE: "…as I see fit" continues to carry the understanding that play activities are limited to those the two of them have already negotiated.)

The Dom may now wish to add some personalized message, such as:

"I want you to know how proud I am of you for being willing to experience these sensations with me; these are new to you and I know that our time together tonight means a lot to you." (You'll have to make it sound like you, of course. I realize I'm a bit stiff when it comes to this sort of thing.)

Play begins

Get Connected. Use as many of the five senses as you can...

* Touch: what have you negotiated?
* Sound: music? (If music, I strongly advise **against** music with words. Personally, I tend towards Japanese Taiko drummers, Australian didgeridoo, or Scottish bagpipe music—it's all eerie, unusual, and somewhat disorienting and thus adds a sense of mystery to the scene. Also—importantly—these all have heavy beats that can help you time your play. When you strike a person in time to music, it can help them to go into trance—which is, for many, part of the path to subspace.)
* Sight, eyes open: What can she see? Does her view augment the scene? Does it help build psychological tension?
* Sight, eyes closed: If the area is bright, I'd suggest a blindfold simply to remove the distraction of bright light; if you're playing in dim light, it's up to you. However, once blindfolded, you can no longer see/monitor her eyes for reactions, so you're taking away one of the ways that you're able to communicate and read the bottom.
* Breath: You can learn to direct your bottom's breathing rate by matching hers and then changing yours subtly and slowly.
* Smell: Incense or scented candles?

Focus on reading the bottom...

(The more you know of this, the better.)

- What sounds is she making? Does it sound as though she's emotionally involved with the play or still in her head? High- pitched sounds generally indicate the person is in their *head* while low-pitched sounds generally indicate the person is responding from their gut or *visceral core*. The more the sensations are new, the more she'll stay in her head as she tries to interpret whether she likes or dislikes the sensations.

- Is she moving her body (or part of their body) toward or away from you? If she seems to be moving *away* from you, I'd suggest that you come present and check for other possible signs that what you are doing with this person is not being well received.

- What's going on with hands/fingers and feet/toes? A e her fingers relaxed or pointed straight out? Hands clenched or open? Legs relaxed or flexed? Toes relaxed or curled? (As behaviors such as these are highly individualized, Tops have to learn what these signals mean for each person with whom they play.)

- Color of fingers/toes (particularly if bondage or inversion is involved): pink, red, purple. NOTE: You can use a simple test for what is called *capillary refill response.* If the bottom's fingernails (or toes) a e unpainted, squeeze the tip until they turn white, release the pressure and judge the time required for the finger or toe to regain proper pinkness. If it takes more than two seconds, you may have a circulation problem. If painted, judge it from the pad of the finger.

- What is her breathing pattern? Deep and slow (relaxed) or rapid and shallow (upset or excited or about to climax). Holding her breath? (Some women hold their breath just as they are about to climax. Depending upon how sadistic you are, you can use this signal to interrupt her orgasm as part of orgasm-denial training.)

- Responsiveness: If you're worried that your bottom is not responding as you had expected, check in. Is the bottom still connected with your play? If not, why not? Has something happened to snap the bottom out of headspace (such as a traumatic flashback)? Does the bottom have anything to tell you (such as, "The knot you tied in the middle of my back is annoying me and bringing me out of my headspace.")?

Technique reminder for Tops: (I know, I keep saying this; it's important.) Should your bottom start to go into subspace, you have to be careful not to do anything (or say anything) that would cause them to think. As previously covered, when someone goes into subspace, they are floating among their feelings. If you ask them a question or do something that is jarring, you'll pull them into their head (thinking state) as they try to figure out what you said or what is happening. It can be a scene-stopper.

But—you may *want* a "scene-stopper." Not all scenes are intended to end with the bottom in subspace. In *tease and denial* scenes, for example, orgasm is not the goal. The goal is to frustrate the bottom by preventing them from reaching their orgasm or teaching them how to control their own sexual response through "edging".

Keep the bottom from becoming desensitized. Sometimes you want to keep repeating a pattern without stopping to produce a cathartic climax or to produce intense pain; other times you want to change what you're doing in order to continue building the overall scene. You will develop your own techniques as you gain experience and confidence in your SM play; here, I'll share some of mine:

- Consider throwing startling sensations into the scene to help disorient the bottom
  - Spray water on their back
  - Use a large piece of tanned leather hide as flogger
  - Slap with the flat of your hands, fingers splayed— lots of noise and not much pain
  - Set off a stun-gun—either in the air for the alarming

sound, or on their body for a totally unexpected sensation

- Use various sounds/patterns to deepen the trance
  - ◦ Fast to slow to quiet
  - ◦ Rattlesnake sound (rain stick or other musical rattling sound)

Play scene ends

Ending styles vary, but (as I've already mentioned a time or two) you want to avoid a sudden stop—too jarring and psychologically upsetting for the bottom. Also, suddenly stopping a scene is not proper BDSM etiquette. You're in control; you need to demonstrate that you're the one who purposefully ended the scene just when you wanted it to end.

Being prepared for the scene to end also means that you've thought ahead and know that the bottom may be cold now that

---

In Top/bottom play, if you've been playing with a submissive bottom (as opposed to Topping another Dominant) it is important to return power back to them lest they now look to you as being THEIR Dom/me as opposed to being a Dom/me with whom they just had a scene.

As I say repeatedly throughout this book, BDSM scenes are intensely emotional and create very strong bonds between people. You can use them intentionally and with integrity to supercharge your relationship or you can use them carelessly and risk causing emotional damage.

Your reputation will not long survive in this community if you become known for emotionally damaging people.

---

the scene is over. So, you have a blanket or towel or robe packed in with your toys. And, you also should have a bottle of water handy, or plan on asking someone nearby to bring you some water. It's important to rehydrate during and after a play scene.

NOTE: It's important to bring some covering wrap, as your bottom is now naked (in public) and may feel emotionally vulnerable. A blanket/ robe symbolically continues the concept of bondage or swaddling (tightly wrapping someone).

Reminders of things I've said earlier in this book:

- Don't play for 40 minutes and then continue to occupy the play space for another 20 minutes cuddling the bottom; it's not appropriate, as others are waiting for that space for their own play. Similarly, don't continue to stand in or very near the play station coiling your bondage rope (or carefully putting toys away). You're preventing the next participants from starting their own scene.

- The bottom's recovery time depends on whether they entered subspace—or on the depth of their submersion into subspace. If you've just completed a heavy scene that dropped the bottom into a long period of subspace, you'll want to plan on spending 20+ minutes of aftercare.

- Once your scene has ended, it is the Top's responsibility to be sure that the area is cleaned up and the play furniture is wiped down.

Closing ritual—after the bottom is up and about

I'm about to give you a simple example of a closing ritual. This example applies mainly to people who are new to BDSM and have a *play* relationship—that is, they are *not* in a D/s or M/s dynamic with one another. Just for the record, in M/s or D/s relationships, the sub generally returns to *service mode* once their scene has ended.

*****

If you began the scene with an opening procedure designed to establish your dominance, I recommend that you consider some kind of closing procedure that brings the bottom solidly back to equality. I recommend this, because a firm closing procedure clearly ends any power exchange that you used to begin the scene and offers the Top a chance to say supportive and positive things to the bottom. I suggest that you insert this ritual after you (the Top) have performed aftercare but before the scene is cleaned up. So, if the scene began with an embrace, you can now repeat that embrace and say something like this:

"tina, you did a great job as my bottom and I hope that we get the opportunity to play again sometime. Thank you again for this scene—I truly enjoyed it. If you're okay to walk now, I'd appreciate your help putting our things away and cleaning up the area, then I'll meet you out in the socializing area so we can visit."

Please realize that some people are more susceptible to trance states than others, and for some people, such a ceremony will have no effect whatsoever. There will be a range of reactions from those with whom you are scening.

Earlier, I mentioned that when you are starting out in this culture, *power exchange* is generally seen as a temporary state.

Two people get together as equals and agree to have a BDSM scene with define boundaries. The bottom surrenders power to the Top for the duration of the scene. Afterwards, the Top returns the bottom's power. Two people of equal personal power go on to have a lovely evening. Power exchange for the purpose of a scene is seen to have a beginning, a middle, and an end.

Now, if this person is not *your own* submissive, the closing ceremony must be designed to leave no doubt that they do not belong to *you*. If this bottom belongs to someone else, courtesy requires you to return the undamaged bottom to their rightful partner and thank that person for permitting you to play with them.

If your bottom is your own submissive, the closing scene can represent a transition away from the play area and back to the social area.

Debriefing and scene report

Earlier, I described these final stages of he overall scene in detail. You should plan on contacting your play partner a few days after the scene to hear their reactions. Remember, it's important not to lead the de-briefing; let them give you the scene report from their point of view. Be careful to listen with an open heart, as you can learn a great deal about yourself, your play partner, and your own reputation.

Chapter 8
The Short Chapter

I'm going to begin the wrap-up by reviewing some of the more important points I've been weaving throughout this book. From there, I'm going to spend just a few pages giving you another way of connecting all the dots. Finally, I'll say goodbye to you and wish you well on your journey—it's quite a journey!

Reiterating key points from this book

Topping and bottoming

During intense scenes, Topping often produces adrenaline while bottoming often causes the brain to release a mix of endorphins and adrenaline (depending on what the Top is doing to the bottom). The fight-o -flight reaction to adrenaline release is relevant to the Top/bottom experience. The unfettered Top may be in an adrenaline-produced *fight* headspace while the (often bound) bottom can be in an adrenaline-induced *flight* headspace that then could cause their brain to release endorphins when the bottom's brain cannot find an escape option for them. The result is that the Top is *in the zone* and the bottom is *in subspace*. As a Top, you'll know you've reached skill- mastery when this process—the ability to control your headspace while dropping a bottom into subspace—becomes a "defined repeatable process" (whether or not your bottom is a regular play partner).

Skill mastery and safety

Skill mastery and safety should be your primary concerns. As my partner, Jen, frequently points out in our lectures, you must absolutely master skills and safety in order to learn how to work with your bottom to move your connection to the spiritual level. We tend to get wrapped up in the skills and techniques of BDSM and forget why we are learning them in the first place. SM is simply another way to interact and connect with another person. Learn your skills and hone your techniques and, once mastered, apply these skills to give one another ecstatic experiences beyond recounting.

Scenes are intense experiences

Intense scenes tend to close the distance between people. They are intimate, authentic, unprotected, vulnerable, naked experiences. When you first start playing, the vulnerability can be a psychological hurdle. The bottom is usually naked while the Top is usually clothed; that's quite a psychological hurdle in its own right, as it's contrary to most vanilla party experiences. Frequently, the bottom is having a new experience while the experienced Top is plying a skill he knows well; this experience-disparity adds to the bottom's sense of unbalance and vulnerability.

Remember, this is the world of tolerance and acceptance. Just because it isn't your kink doesn't make it *less than* your kink. One person's *icky* is another person's *mmm*!

Sometimes, negotiating for a scene reveals mismatches

Sometimes, when you are negotiating for a scene, you'll have a sense that you're just not the right Top/bottom for this person. It's okay to say "no" to someone. You don't have to end up playing together just because you begin negotiating with them. Sometimes the Top has to have the presence to withdraw; sometimes it is the bottom that must withdraw.

Before I learned this lesson, I once had a negotiation that revealed that the lady and I had nearly polar views about what I was offering and what was going to be okay with her. We had the scene, but we have not said a word to one another since then. That was in 2008. Not a great outcome. From this experience, I learned to use exit cues such as: "When I play with someone, my intention is to give them the best scene that I can. From what I can tell by our conversation, our fetishes (or play styles or wants/needs) don't match very well. Perhaps we should find others who are a better fit. But, I'm drawn to you; would you like to go out for a cup of coffee?"

Some new ideas to consider

Trust in play

Few people think about *trust* *i*n play as it relates to the Top *trusting* the bottom beyond the obvious—that the Top trusts that the bottom will use safewords when needed.

But, there is more to it than that. The Top must trust that the bottom will be clear with them about their own scene needs. Bottoms that simply go along with whatever the Top wants to dish out may not be getting their own wants/needs met. That leads down the path that raises two questions:

- Does the bottom even know what they want from that particular scene or Top?
- Pragmatically, how does the bottom communicate *more* or *harder* feedback during an ongoing scene?

While the answer to the first question is relatively easy—have more and varied experiences in order to have a better understanding of

what they do and do not like—the answer to the second question
can hold hidden surprises. The way that the bottom asks for *more*
depends upon the scene and the Top's personality. Just imagine a
Top's reaction to each of these two sentences:

- First option, respectful: "Sir, with respect, Sir, I can take that harder, Sir."
- Second option, bratty: "Sheesh! You hit like my sister! Who taught you to throw that flogger?" and so for h.

While the respectful request will likely result in the Top gradually
increasing the sensation while monitoring the bottom's reactions,
the bratty request is likely to cause the Top immediately to ratchet
up the play intensity by quite a bit—or cause them to stop the
scene entirely because of the bottom's disrespect.

Most Tops take themselves and their scening quite seriously and
will be pissed off with any form of Topping from the bottom. Oh,
and you also risk getting tagged as a SAM—smart-assed masochist.

Within our widely ranging community, the topic of *brattiness* comes
up every so often because there is a substantial subculture of folks
called *spankos* who have eroticized spankings. In the spanko
community *brattiness* is a standard and accepted part of their play
(and is on full display during spanko parties). A *brat* will be *bratty*
in order to provoke someone into spanking them—which, in turn,
fulfills their needs.

Many times, I've seen a spanko bottom who is having a lot of fun
at a BDSM party drop some of their guards and be bratty to a non-
spanko Dom/me who isn't the least bit amused. *Bratty* sometimes
conflict with BDSM scening.

So, back to trust and honesty. Ultimately, each partner must know
themselves and their needs well enough to know what to ask for
and how to ask for it so that both the Top and bottom are playing
within their skill levels while getting their mutual needs met.

Doing it the *right* way

Some people—whether new or established within the BDSM culture— seem to think that what they have read or been told is some kind of *Rulebook of Kinky Behavior* that they and others should be following. These people seem to think that when they see someone acting in a way they would not have expected (or read about or been told by someone else), that this other person is doing it *wrong*. It could be, and I encourage these people to (unobtrusively) ask someone more experienced about it. However, it's more likely that the person they're observing simply does X differently than they've experienced. No more, no less, just different.

PhoenixRed has pointed out that while there certainly can be *safe* and *unsafe* ways of doing things in SM play, *rightness* and *wrongness* become blurred when it comes to BDSM topics in general and SM play styles, in particular. However, some people remain remarkably uninfluenced by reason and logic and believe so strongly in their own views about what is right or wrong that they offer unsolicited opinions about how others should behave. Sooner or later, you'll hear such phrases as, "He doesn't act like a *real* Dom," or "Girl, you need to read 'The Ninefold Path to Submission' to learn how to act."

Hmmmm.

"Pot, kettle here—checking in, Pot; is everything still black over where you are?"

We're all kinky—and some of us are kinky in ways that make other kinksters uncomfortable. If you're hearing about (or seeing) some form of BDSM that you find revolting or disturbing, please keep you're your opinions to yourself. Give others their own opportunities to be weird.

As another saying goes, when you're pointing your forefinger at someone, your four other fingers are pointing back at you. When you hear someone criticizing someone else, you might wish to pause and consider a few things about the person offering their critical opinion:

- What are the grounds of their authority?
- Is their authority earned or self-declared?
- What personal insecurities might have been triggered for them to be saying what they're saying?
- What do they have to gain by telling you this?
- Are they behaving with honor and integrity to be saying what they are saying about another person or situation?

As I said a few paragraphs ago, *rightness* and *wrongness* become blurred when it comes to most of what goes on in BDSM. These values become particularly blurry when it comes to relationship topics. In relationships, whether vanilla or kinky, some personal behaviors support relationships better than others, but you're not going to know whether those behaviors are right or wrong until the relationship is shown to succeed or fail. And even then, whether or not a relationship held together or split apart, who are we, as outsiders, to judge how the participants felt about it? I have certainly been in relationships that did not last but that served to teach me (and my partner) some *very* valuable lessons that we would not otherwise have learned—and that have subsequently helped us in other relationships.

So… here's an easy test to apply to your own relationships to know whether they're right or wrong for you: ask yourself how happy you are with your own friends or partner(s). If you like the answers, you're doing just fine. If you don't like the answers, then remember this. You're the only one in charge of you; you are the only one who can change *you*. You can't change the other person, you can only change your *reaction* to the other person. As you change your reaction to *them*, they will change their reactions to *you*. This is probably what you sought in the first place, but you may not have quite understood that it's your move, not theirs.

The tyranny of technique

There is a scene in the 1981 movie *Raiders of the Lost Ark* where Harrison Ford (as Indiana Jones) is running through a bazaar in

Cairo trying to find Marion (who has been kidnapped by some Nazis) when he suddenly comes face-to-face with a sinister smiling villain dressed in a black robe who is making very complex and threatening motions with a scimitar. Indiana Jones freezes in his tracks as he tries to understand what he's seeing. After watching the guy for a second or two, Indy straightens up, shrugs, pulls out his pistol, and shoots the guy dead from about 20 paces.

Now, take that situation into the dungeon. Sooner or later, you're going to see a Top who seems to be **performing** for those who are watching as opposed to **connecting** with the bottom—or even connecting with their own sadistic pleasure. In a general way, there is a tendency among those new to BDSM to mistake form for substance. They think, for example, that a flogging scene is about flogging; it can take many years before some Tops realize that a scene is about *connecting* with the bottom or with their own passions—and that floggers (as an example) are simply one of the many useful tools of the trade.

By this point in the book, it should come as no surprise to learn that newcomers will be awarded the most credit by senior BDSMers by demonstrating their ability to correctly "read" and connect with their bottom while safely using their newly-learned SM techniques. The test of that (or any other) scene is determined by the quality of the "ride" that they share with their partners.

The tyranny of technique poses another risk, too. This state of affairs (performing rather than connecting) can lead to what I call *unconscious play*. Unconscious play (the opposite of *mindful play*) can be seen in a Top or bottom whose attention is divided between the activities occurring within the scene and some kind of distracted behavior—for example, looking around the room to see who's watching. Unconscious play can be seen in the emotionally detached bottom whose reactions don't correspond to the Top's actions, and unconscious play can be seen in the emotionally detached Top who seems to be going through the passionless motions of some SM technique. (As in bad sex, they're faking it, and it shows.)

Pageantry as state change

Pageantry: the U.S. Marine Corps Band starts to play *Hail to the Chief* as the President enters a room. Everybody in the hushed auditorium stands and applauds when the highly regarded guest speaker walks to the podium. Those seated at the dinner table all wait politely as the host lifts his glass to offer a toast. *Pageantry.*

Pageantry is the *getting ready* process that starts to shift your headspace for the beginning of a scene. It can be a kink scene in a dungeon, the scene that you've worked out for a hot date, or a personal scene that you go through before you start work each day (like a meditation). I encourage you to think about how you might use pageantry to add some sparkle and creativity into your relationships.

How a great scene can go bad

I've described scenes as playing with SM sensations and/or playing with power exchange. For this section, I'm going to switch to Dom/sub from Top/bottom because what I'm describing has a psychological component and applies to D/s SM play—Dominants of either gender, of course.

People seldom discuss scenes in relation to playing with *vulnerability*. But, when you think about it, it makes sense: for the bottom to take the ride, they must open themselves physically and emotionally to be receptive to the sensations at the same time that the Top has to know how to read the bottom *and also* be emotionally receptive in order that the two people can have a good energy exchange.

In this book, I've given you quite a bit of detail about the mechanics of setting up SM play scenes that could go beyond the limits of ordinary experience in order to make lasting memories. But, these extraordinary scenes are not without the potential for some risk.

Guy Baldwin first introduced me to the possibility of psychological risk in his book *Ties that Bind.* He commented that the path to transcendence in BDSM involves stressing the mind through power exchange (D/s) and stressing the body through SM practices. Guy, a practicing psychotherapist, observed that when one is involved in a scene at this level of concentration and focus, unanticipated risks materialize. These risks include a narrowing of the Top's visual focus and a lessening of the Top's (and bottom's) ability to hear sounds around not directly related to the scene. Partly, this is because the Top is *in the zone* and it's partly because both people are responding to their environment from within their core emotions. Once there, both the Top and bottom are in a kind of trance state. Like all trance states, it can be difficult to know whether or not you're in one. If you've ever driven past your freeway exit, you've had the experience of being in a trance state without realizing it. Daydreaming is a trance state.

Scene-induced trance states can leave both the conscious and unconscious mind less well defended than usual. You are more at risk than at most other times specifically because you don't realize that your mind needs defending. You're simply not sufficiently self-aware to know that you need to be mentally on guard. In this condition, people may be much more vulnerable than they realize or intend. Worse, this unguarded trance state can be a pathway for unusual ideas, ideas that twist, change, and alter your sense of reality in unknowable ways.

At these times, there is a risk that the Top or bottom—in their altered mental state—may misinterpret some of the sensory inputs swirling around them (e.g., people speaking, wrong kind of music, etc.) and overreact. Some interruption or disharmony that might normally be a nonevent can escalate into a very real and significant event. The scene can explode without either the Top or bottom quite understanding what happened to set it off.

But wait, there is more. Let's say the scene went just fine and now you're giving or receiving aftercare. You're not quite out of the risk-zone. The trance state—that state that you may not realize you're in—can continue past the SM play and linger during aftercare. When this happens, the after-scene conversation can carry some unusual risks. For example, let's say that one partner was experienced and the other is pretty new to SM play. Let's say that one partner had a really good time but the other person just didn't quite connect. If, during the emotionally fragile period following play when one or both of you are still coming out of your trance states, the elated person turns enthusiastically to the other and asks, "What did you think of our scene?" a casual reply such as, "Not much, I've had better," may be more emotionally damaging than you'd expect—because of the light trance state. A casual comment during aftercare has the potential to plant an extremely positive or negative idea in someone's mind that they remember for years. It may very well cause the excited partner to associate SM play—at least SM play with this particular person—with great personal success or great personal failure.

If a negative experience of this kind happens early in a newcomer's exposure to BDSM, they may withdraw from the community permanently with extremely negative feelings about it.

But wait, there is still more.

Let's say that the scene ended beautifully. The Dom/me emotionally supported the sub; the sub expressed his/her pleasure and gratitude to the Dom/me. There even was a closing ceremony during which the Dom/me returned the sub's personal power. They did everything right according to conventional wisdom. What might be wrong with this picture?

What might be wrong is called *The Invisible Collar*.

The Invisible Collar

My partner and co-author created the term *invisible collar* to describe the lingering emotional connection between people after an emotionally bonding experience that does not end decisively. It doesn't matter whether the emotionally bonding experience is a single intense scene or a months- or years-long intense personal relationship. What seems to matter is that there was not a clearly understood end.

She coined the phrase after recognizing some common patterns emerging from discussions about M/s relationship break-ups. In particular, Jen noticed that people who had been involved in intense relationships that had ended with *closure* reported very different post- relationship experiences than did people whose relationships had just fizzled away.

While *huge* emotional pain and trauma often comes with the end of relationships, it seemed that people got over their break-ups much faster when those relationships had been ended with dignity and formality. In fact, many people admitted that when they had been in relationships that had ended without closure, they often felt a lingering connection that could last for many months or even years. During that agonizing time of unresolved separation, one or both of the previous partners would want to call/contact/reach out to the other person. Many people said they continued to think about the way the relationship ended and wished they could have done something different to have prevented the break-up. These people reported that the other person was often on their mind and that this period was a slow emotional torture.

Jen coined the term *invisible collar* to describe the long-lasting tug (or pull) towards a prior relationship partner long after they had expected those feelings to go away. She and I discussed the concept quite a bit and realized that the *invisible collar* concept ties in with the way one ends a scene with people other than regular committed partners.

- You enter an interaction (either for a meeting, a scene, or even a brief relationship) with purpose and intent.
- When the meeting/scene/relationship is over, you either have or have not fulfilled your purpose and intent.
- To the extent that something is left unfinished, to the extent that you feel that the connection did not resolve completely, you may be left with a *psychological connection* that may take longer to fade than you expected.

That's the Invisible Collar.

Putting all this into a business-planning perspective

Well, you've almost finished this book. That's a good thing, for this book should have given you the information to help you play safely with others. As I mentioned at the start of Chapter 1, this book offers Tops the wisdom to know how to proceed ethically in our community and it offers bottoms the knowledge about how to play safely. More now than when you started this book, I suspect that you realize that there is a lot going on in a culture you'd barely heard about before.

I'm going to take these last few pages to string this BDSM material together differently than I have up to this point. I'm doing this because people get "Aha!" moments when material clicks in a certain way for them, and this is a very different way of piecing the BDSM puzzle together.

I've created an outline of a mini business plan as though you were going to set out on a Quest to learn about—and participate in—the world of BDSM.

Phase One: Gather Information

- Study the relevant literature: Read books about BDSM.
- Study examples in practice: Go to munches and play parties, speak with those who have gone before you, but don't get committed.
- Keep a record of experiences: Make notes about what interests you and what does not. Determine the common elements of our likes and dislikes.
- Summarize your finding : Journal, or at least make some notes about what you're finding and of the questions or concerns that you have yet to answer.
- Make a "Go/No-go" decision: Decide whether this is the right path for you.

Phase Two: Determine something about your own needs and limits

- *Develop a needs statement*: Identify what you, yourself, are looking for in this kinky world.

- *Understand the rules of the game*: Learn safe and unsafe *SM techniques*, *players*, and *play styles*.

- *Develop screening criteria for partners*: Look at your past dating choices—are you happy with them? Are there any particular wants and/or needs that you would prefer in a partner— whether or not a play partner? Any specific demographics or physical traits?

Phase Three: Select Candidates

- *Interview candidates:* When you find someone who appears to be interested in you at a munch or play party, ask them to explain themselves. Ask about their BDSM experiences, what clubs they belong to, how much public play they've had, what books they've read, what workshops or courses they've had, etc. Everyone has to start somewhere, so some people may not yet have built up much of a background. That's understandable; I'm only suggesting that if they're new to this, you need to know that they're new (especially if they're claiming to know all about it). There's nothing quite so potentially dangerous as the person who claims to have been into BDSM for a few years yet admits that no, they haven't read any books about BDSM nor attended any education classes sponsored by local clubs, and for whom the word *Mentor* might as well be the name of a Greek ship.

- *Ask others about the prospect*: Ask more experienced club members about the person or people you're interested in befriending.

Phase Four: Extend a Play Offer

- *Be prepared to say "No" to a suitor*: Pay attention to your gut instincts. If someone is trying to overwhelm you with their experience and knowledge, check around with others (is this person for real or are they a legend in their own minds?).

So, now compare this kind of planned approach to entering BDSM to the more common strategy called *muddling through.*

Some people—mostly young men, in my experience—resist study and planning in most areas of their lives. They have a job (as opposed to a career); they have a girlfriend (or wife, so they're getting laid), and they eat food (unceremoniously). Unfortunately, in intense BDSM relationships, failure to plan usually results in failure to launch. It can be hard for those who are new to BDSM to understand/interpret the actions/reactions of someone who has entered this culture yet has declined to read books or attend lectures and workshops. These people appear to be part of the local scene; they appear to fit in well with others—but they're causing problems. They don't know what they don't know and when they get into BDSM clubs or personal relationships they try to work themselves out of trouble that wouldn't have happened had they known more about BDSM or about relationship management.

Over my years as a volunteer on allexperts.com, I've frequently heard from people who are trying to grapple with confusing problems that crop up within their D/s or M/s relationships. One of the most common situations runs like this…

They've been in a relationship for a fairly short time, say 2–6 months. They have found real-time BDSM after some period in BDSM chat rooms. They're in a self-declared Dom/sub or Master/slave structure. They don't know much about D/s or M/s; they have not read books on those subjects; they seldom belong to a BDSM club. They're winging it, making it up as they go along. The Dom/Master is telling the sub/slave that he's training her for his pleasure, but she doesn't quite get it; she's an electrical engineering student— why should he be training her about how to set the table. You sense that this relationship is not heading in a good direction.

In the business world, there is a kind of non-training cycle that is sometimes cynically referred to as *the mushroom-growing approach to staff development*: throw them in the closet, shovel manure on top, leave them alone and see what happens. This applies to BDSM-based relationships that are being "led" by a person who discounts formal learning in favor of a trial-and-error approach. This is the approach taken by the person who would say, "I'm not much of a reader, I'm more of a doer." Yeah, right.

My advice to the submissive partner in such a relationship is to stop, take a deep breath, and seriously assess your situation. Your own long-term mental health may benefit from moving on to find someone who knows a thing or two about BDSM theory and practice, team leadership, and teaching strategies.

I was recently discussing with PhoenixRed the issue of people playing in the BDSM world yet not reading the existing literature. She commented that she sees this behavior mostly from male/female subs who seem to cloak themselves in the mantle of, "You're the Dom, you're supposed to teach me everything you want me to know, right?"

If you're interested in reading a book designed to give you the same kind of bullet-proofing for relationship issues that this book gives you for BDSM play, parties, and scene protocols, then I again would point you to our next book in this series. It's titled: *BDSM Mastery— Relationships: a guide for creating mindful relationships for Dominants and submissives.*

Wishing you the very best

Before I leave you, let me caution you again as I did in the introduction. A decision to participate in the BDSM way of life is a decision to be transformed in some way. Some will be careful and fortunate and will be rewarded by finding what Guy Baldwin refers to as *ecstatic erotic catharsis*. Some will find themselves caught up in intense relationships, yet—over time—discover that their reasons for participating in this edgy form of sexuality are not good reasons. Some will *not* take to heart the guidance, cautions,

Chapter 8—The Short Chapter

and admonitions that you've been reading in this book and will, unfortunately, discover that their participation in the BDSM community has actually made them more wary and less trusting of others and may cause them to leave the BDSM world more isolated and miserable than they were initially.

Please be aware: While most who enter find a welcome home, others who enter are not as fortunate. As with most complex projects, the more time and effort you put into studying and exploring, the more you'll get out of it.

Which brings us to a central truth about being a human: In your life, progress is a choice. You can stay intellectually, emotionally, socially, physically, and fiscally as you are, or you can choose to continue to learn and grow. Personal growth is just that—personal. The aphorism that expresses this thought so succinctly is: *If it's going to be, it's up to me.*

You've been exposed to a lot of material in this book and it's likely to take you some time to digest it. I've included some supplementary material to help point you to other valuable resources. I hope that you feel more comfortable about the world of BDSM since reading this book, for that has been our goal.

May the wind be always at your back.

In Leather Heart and Spirit,

Bob and Jen

Supplements

Supplement A: Glossary of terms

Aftercare: A scene doesn't end when the toys are put away. Aftercare describes a period at the close of a scene when each partner can reaffirm the other as they regain physical and mental control of themselves.

Authority-based relationships: Relationships where one person is clearly the leader and the other is clearly subordinate. Among the more common structures listed here, this book mostly describes D/s relationships.

- Dominant/submissive (D/s)
- Master/slave (M/s)
- Owner/property (O/p)
- TPE (Total Power Exchange).

BDSM: represents a continuum of practices and expressions, both erotic and non-erotic, involving restraint, sensory stimulation, role- playing, and a variety of interpersonal dynamics. The term "BDSM" is an abbreviation of: **B**ondage/**D**iscipline; **D**ominance/ submission; **S**ado**M**asochism.

bottom: the person *receiving* the action (see also: Top)

Dominant **and** ***submissive:*** (**Dom** and **sub** or **D-type** and **s-type**) are terms that relate to behaviors linked to personality traits; you could as easily substitute the terms *leader* and *follower*.

Dom and Domme: the shorthand male and female version of the word *dominant*. Generally, when I write "Dom" the person can be of either gender. When the topic specifically concerns a female dominant I will use "Domme." A female dominant is not to be confused with a domineering female. A domineering female (sometimes called a *bitch*) **expects** service while a dominant of either gender **accepts** service in the context of their role as the dominant leader.

D/s play or D/s scenes: D/s play includes the power exchange component along with SM tools/toys

D/s scenes with sadistic/masochistic preferences–Combining: A dominant (Dom or D-type) and a submissive (sub or s-type) may have either sadistic or masochistic erotic preferences. Most commonly, those with dominant personalities give strong sensations to others, but every so often you will find a strong D-type who has connected sexual pleasure from receiving those strong (possibly painful) sensations.

Dungeon Monitor (DM): A Dungeon Monitor (sometimes referred to as a Dungeon Master or simply a DM) is a person charged with supervising a playspace (or dungeon) at BDSM events such as play parties and fetish clubs. While on duty they monitor the safety of all participants and their authority is absolute. They can stop your scene; they can have you removed from the party.

Edging: A sexual D/s term meaning the act of bringing a man or woman up to the edge of orgasm and then keeping them there— often as they are begging for release.

Edgeplay: This word is used in two ways: first, to refer to SM play that is on the edge of someone's personal limits; and second, to refer to SM play that falls into one of two categories

- Category one—requires advanced training: "You'd better be well trained before you try this one."
- Category two—it's seriously taboo: "You'd better lower your voice before discussing that one."

Emotional Triggers (Landmines): Words or situations that cause an unexpected and often emotionally intense reaction in someone that developed from prior (and often suppressed) traumatic experiences.

Extremeaphiles: People who love to play on the edge.

Gor: short for *Gorean*—a subculture that grew out of the science fiction novels of John Norman based on a belief that in the natural order, all males are inherently dominant over all females. There are communities of people who live according to Gorean customs much as there are communities of people who live according to some aspect of BDSM customs.

Hurt vs. harm: For the sake of this book, *hurt* is "ouch" but *harm* can last a lifetime. Thus, the sentence "I will be glad to hurt you if you'd like, but I definitely do not wish to harm you" makes sense. In your mind, you can substitute the phrase *intense sensations* for "hurt."

Kinky: slang for *people who enjoy adventuresome sex* which is, itself, a euphemism for BDSM. (Note: Some BDSM relationships can be mostly about discipline and non-sexual aspects of domination and service submission. This distinguishes such relationships from those in the vanilla world.)

Kinsey scale: The 0-6 Kinsey scale (also called the Heterosexual-Homosexual Rating Scale) attempts to describe a person's sexual preferences. In this scale, zero means that the person is exclusively heterosexual and six means that the person is exclusively homosexual. Someone who is bisexual would be a 3.

Leather, Leathermen, Leathersex: The Leather subculture is one of many facets of semi-organized alternative sexuality. In recent decades the Leather community has almost come to be viewed as a subset of BDSM culture rather than a descendant of gay culture. Almost anything that is said about Leather and its evolution to present times is subject to challenge.

Limits: Boundaries negotiated between the Top and bottom before a scene. Hard limits represent "do not do these" topics; soft limits represent "I'd rather you not do these" topics.

Masochism: in psychiatry, the condition in which sexual gratification depends on suffering physical pain or humiliation; gratification gained from pain, deprivation, degradation, etc., inflicted or imposed on oneself, either as a result of one's own actions or the actions of others, especially the tendency to seek this form of gratification.

Master and slave: usually applied to a 24/7 relationship structure wherein the subordinate person (slave) has surrendered authority over themselves and pledged to serve and to obey their Master who now exerts total control and offers total protection for this person.

Munch: Munches are intended to be non-threatening social gatherings to help those who are curious about BDSM meet others who may be able to help them become more comfortable and better informed. Munches can also be a place to get advice about BDSM experiences.

Negotiating/negotiations: The process of determining what will and will not go on in a play scene—or in a relationship. As some people consider the scene to start with negotiations, this is not a time to be interrupted.

Old Guard: A term used to describe a near-mythical time in gay Leather history when returned GIs from World War II blended some features of their military experiences with their kinky interests to produce a subculture that over time became known as *Leather*. Some of the distant echoes of their quasi-military rules of protocol, inclusion, and exclusion can still be seen in today's BDSM society.

Pansexual: accepting of all sexual orientations—generally referring to social clubs (as opposed to clubs that primarily welcome straights, gay males, people who are genetically female, etc.).

RACK: Risk Aware Consensual Kink—a standard of play different from SSC that you will run into as you get more experience under your belt.

Sadism: in psychiatry, the condition in which sexual gratification depends on causing pain or degradation to others.

SM: sadomasochism (I use caps for these letters in this book). The psychological tendency or sexual practice characterized by both sadism and masochism.

SM play/scenes: activities between two or more people of any gender that involve giving and receiving sensations such as spanking, flogging whipping, etc. for their mutual and consensual enjoyment.

SM techniques: methods such as spanking, whipping, bondage, or electro-stimulation that sadists may use to cause masochists to feel the desired sensations.

SSC: Safe, Sane, and Consensual—A slogan used to summarize the minimal physical/psychological conditions most people consider acceptable for SM play to take place.

Safe-call: a procedure used when meeting someone for the firs time (or even when meeting someone that you don't know well) that ensures that someone else knows what you're doing, where you'll be doing it, and that you are safe.

Safewords: words that you and your partner have agreed to use to stop the play entirely (such as, *red*), or to slow it down a bit (such as, *yellow*). One uses words such as *red* because words such as, "No" or "Stop" or "Ouch, no, stop!" may be part of the scene.

Service Top: someone who has developed the skills to administer SM sensations to a bottom and does so at that person's request. A service Top's intent is to fulfill the wishes and desires of the person bottoming for them. Even though a service Top may not dominate the scene in terms of a D/s dynamic, they do control the scene. As the phrase implies, the Top is doing something for the sake of the bottom.

Sex-role stereotyping: the general public stereotype is that Doms are men with sadistic/Top preferences and that submissives are women who have masochistic/bottom preferences. These are stereotypes and are far from the way roles are practiced within this culture. In reality, Dominants can be male or female, masochists or sadists and of any sexual orientation. So can submissives.

Supplement A—Glossary of Terms

Submissive vs. slave

Note: Once again, I caution readers that the characteristics listed under *submissive* and *slave* are generalizations based on my own research and experiences living within (and studying) the field of BDSM and Master/slave relations since 2001. These descriptions are certainly not intended to be taken as *rules*. These are my own distinctions and may not be generally accepted by others practicing D/s or M/s structures.

As you, yourself, grow in BDSM experience, what I write in this book generally—and the following points about distinctions between *submissive* and *slave* specifically—may make more sense to you.

I'll begin by proposing that *submissive* and *slave* motivations and behaviors aren't quite the same. While one is certainly not better than the other, one set of behaviors is more likely to fit some people than others.

submissive

- D/s relationship is based on power *exchange* (meaning that the submissive who normally has personal authority over what they, themselves, may or may not do or have done to them can give or exchange that power to the Dom/me for a prescribed period)
- Submissives have a strong desire to serve—but under certain negotiated conditions.
- Typically, the negotiated area include the submissive's terms of service, the length of that service, the hard and soft limits, and the safewords.
- The submissive will also negotiate those aspects of their life that the Dom doesn't control. These aspects often include the submissive's biological family and children, work, education and religious observance.
- The conditions under which the submissive is willing to serve can be renegotiated. (This is a major issue: the submissive retains the personal authority to ask their Dominant to

renegotiate their terms of service, but the Dominant is under no obligation to accept the newly proposed conditions.)

- If the Dom breaks the submissive's hard limits, the scene would end and—in the case of a breach of a relationship trust—the relationship could end.

- The Dom may be permitted to break *soft limits* (things the submissive has said they really aren't interested in) after discussing it with the submissive and obtaining their permission.

- In many/most cases, submissives cross back and forth between retaining and surrendering control over some aspect of their lives and continue to make decisions in the areas that are off- limits for their Dom

- A submissive re-submits to the Dom at the start of any scene or activity over which the Dom has negotiated authority. Importantly, the submissive retains the choice as to whether or not to submit to the Dom.

Consensual slave

- M/s relationship is based on authority *transfer* (This means that once the person who is to become the slave has, in fact, surrendered personal authority over him/herself to their Master/Owner, they no longer have the personal power to make decisions for him/herself. Thus, a slave would not have the authority to enter into a D/s scene with someone other than their Master/Owner without that Master/Owner's specifically transferring THEIR authority over their own slave to another person.)

- At least in theory, the slave gives up all rights to make personal decisions and becomes the property of a Master or Owner.

- The core values are *service* and *obedience*.

- The slave loses the right to say "No" to Master: in its place, slave may say, "Sir, if it pleases you, Sir" to mean: "Master, I really rather would not do that." or "Sir, only if it pleases you, Sir" which is as close to "No" as slave is permitted. (Note: Master has an ethical obligation only to push through an "only if" reply so long as Master thinks that doing so remains in the slave's best interest. Requiring a slave to proceed through an "only if" command on Master's whim violates the basic Master/ slave pact on Master's part and represents a contract violation.)

- As slave cannot **red out**, slave thus has accepted their Master's limits and does what is asked of them regardless of their feelings about it. ("What does *liking it* have to do with it?")

- In many cases, a slave will give up their rights to personal property and will continue to work for the benefit of Master's household or business.

- A slave's purpose is to make Master's life easier. In that regard, a slave is expected to know Master's wants and likes to the extent that the slave can take independent action on Master's behalf (proactive rather than reactive; to show initiative as a thinking person)

- If a slave removes their own collar it constitutes withdrawal from the relationship

- May be more interested in taking care of others (service heart) than in being taken care of (*sorts by others* in psychology- speak)

- May very well be a dominant in most other aspects of their life, but have chosen to be submissive to (or simply to serve) one single person

Subspace: Similar to *runner's high*, this is an altered state of mind/ body dissociation, detached from worldly cares that is often obtained by bottoms during and SM play scene. (See also: Top-space)

Switch—common use: someone who enjoys being either the Top or the bottom; enjoys giving or receiving physical SM stimulation. Among Leathermen, activity switches are sometimes referred to as *versatile*.

Switch—less common use: someone who is willing to take either the leadership or subordinate role in a relationship depending upon the *chemistry* or *connection* within that particular partner. When used this way, a person is referred to as a **psychological switch**. (Note: while *physical switches* can easily switch within their relationship, psychological switches do not. Psychological switches would have relationships wherein their roles are different—dominant in one relationship and subordinate (not necessarily submissive) with the other. This is an advanced and controversial topic and I only touch on it in this book.)

Top: the person *doing* the action.

Top/bottom play: sensation play with SM toys/tools—no psychological dynamic, no power exchange. *Top* and *bottom* are terms that relate to physical action only. The Top spanks the bottom. The Top or the bottom may be a dominant person or a submissive person of either gender. *Top* and *bottom* only describe *roles* while *dominant* and *submissive* describe how people interact in relationships. The decision to Top or to bottom is only a decision of which person wishes to receive sensations that the tools/toys produce when handled by someone who has been properly trained.

Topspace: a state of intense focus and concentration sometimes attained by a Top during particularly intense scenes.

Toys/tools: the implements or equipment used in a BDSM scene. By some tradition or other, the Leather community generally refers to this equipment as *tools* while the BDSM community seems to use the term *toys*.

Vanilla: the term used by those of us who practice BDSM sex for those who do not practice BDSM sex. It's not a pejorative term, simply a descriptor. Typical uses: vanilla sex, land of vanillas, etc.

Supplement B: Where to find more information

Lists

- Of practically every kink known to man—just in case you thought you'd heard it all: everything2.com/title/ Submissive+BDSM+Play+Partner+Check+List
- Glossary of BDSM terms: www.xeromag.com/fvbdglossary. html

Major general information resource sites

- www.FetLife.com: "Fet," as it is called, is *the* go-to source for just about anything these days. It is like Facebook for those of us interested in BDSM. There are discussion groups for just about any topic you can think of. It's my first stop for anything I'm researching. (Thanks, John Baku, for creating this website.)
- bannon.com: the site that is both 100% authoritative and responsible. Race Bannon, author of *Learning The Ropes: A Basic Guide to Safe and Fun BDSM Lovemaking* not only sends you to responsible sites but also provides some guidance about what to be looking for and avoiding when it comes to Internet searches concerning BDSM and Leather.
- Extremely useful site for all things submissive: www. submissiveguide.com
- High quality information: www.the-iron-gate.com
- Good information: http://collarncuffs.com/resources/doku. php?id=bdsm
- One of the most comprehensive and sophisticated sites I can recommend—particularly for types of play and the psychology of play—belongs to Peter Masters (Sydney,

AU). Clever guy. www.peter-masters.com/wiki/index.php/
The_ Control_Book

Website links referenced in this book

- For more about SSC, see the essay "Safe Sane Consensual: The evolution of a shibboleth" by david stein. david coined the phrase in the first place. You can download a free PDF from his personal website, boybear.us.

National organizations

- **National Coalition for Sexual Freedom** (NCSF): Formed in 1997, NCSF's goal is to fight for sexual freedom and privacy rights for all adults who engage in safe, sane and consensual behavior. www.ncsfreedom.org
- **The Woodhull Foundation**: The Woodhull Foundation envisions a world that recognizes sexual freedom as the fundamental human right of all individuals to develop and express their unique sexuality. They support personal autonomy with regard to bodily integrity and expression without societal or governmental interference, coercion, or stigmatization. www.woodhullalliance.org

Supplement C: Suggested reading

First, an apology to authors whose works are not listed here. There are so many extraordinarily good books on the market that I've had to force myself to stop listing them here. These books should only represent a starting point for your further reading.

Books if You're Just Starting Out in BDSM

- *Screw the Roses, Send Me the Thorns: The Romance and Sexual Sorcery of Sadomasochism* by Philip Miller and Molly Devon (The classic guide to sadomasochism that is intended to strip away myth, shame, and fear about BDSM to reveal truths about this intense form of eroticism.)
- *When Someone You Love is Kinky* by Dossie Easton and Catherine Liszt (**very** helpful for explaining your interest and involvement in BDSM to non-kinky family and friends.)
- *Sensuous Magic, 2 Edition: Your guide to SM for Adventurous Couples* by Patrick Califia (Califia mixes erotic vignettes with practical advice and personal insights to produce a very creative guide to sadomasochism for couples.)
- *Playing Well with Others* by Lee Harrington and Mollena Williams (Interestingly, this book is a marvelous companion to this book. We cover very little ground in common and their material really picks up where this book has left off. And both authors are friends of mine.)
- *The New Topping Book* by Dossie Easton and Janet W. Hardy (Helps to explain what make someone a **good** Dominant, including some of the mental aspects of being a dominant, offers some advice on BDSM play and techniques, and covers the all-important area of safety.
- *The New Bottoming Book* by Janet W. Hardy and Dossie Easton (The mate to *The New Topping Book*, this one is written for submissives/bottoms and deals largely with the

mental/emotional aspects of being a submissive, rather than hands-on instructions in techniques and toys.)

- *The Ethical Slut* by Dossie Easton (The essential guide for singles and couples who want to explore polyamory in ways that are ethically and emotionally sustainable.)

Books on the Psychological Aspects of BDSM

- *The Control Book* by Peter Masters (One of my favorite books: This book is about the fine art of taking control of your partner, especially such processes as using control, ensuring that you have control, and—importantly—about giving control back once you are done with it. To his vast credit, Masters also discusses how to fix a situation if it goes psychologically wrong.)

- *This Curious Human Phenomenon: An Exploration of Some Uncommonly Explored Aspects of BDSM* by Peter Masters (Masters is one of my heroes. Fabulous author and profound thinker. There is material in this book that you simply won't find addressed by any other author.)

- *Partners in Power: Living in Kinky Relationships* by Jack Rinella (A *must read* before you start a D/s relationship. It addresses the question: "Is it possible to form lasting, healthy, loving relationships that are based on power, control and pain?")

- *The Master's Manual: A Handbook of Erotic Dominance* by Jack Rinella (Another *must read*—particularly if you're starting down the Master/slave path.)

- *Ties That Bind: The SM/Leather/Fetish Erotic Style: Issues, Commentaries and Advice* by Guy Baldwin (A practicing psychologist and one of the most important thinkers on subjects of SM/leather/fetish erotic style, this is a "must read" book covering relationship issues, the Leather community, the SM experience, and personal transformation, as they relate to this form of erotic play).

Supplement D: Acknowledgments

I particularly want to thank my partner and Owner, M. Jen Fairfield for her extensive help and support during the many months that it has taken to complete this work. This book could not possibly be what it now has become without her extensive guidance and profound understanding of BDSM in general and authority-based relationships in particular.

As often as not, Jen influenced and shaped the ideas that now comprise this book. In order to become an expert in this field, she read dozens of books by virtually every authority in this area of expertise in order to find and to pass on to me some of the important supporting information that has rounded out this work. Also, she takes great notes in BDSM classes at weekend conferences.

In addition to helping me with content and flow, Jen made sure that I had the time I needed to write this book—an important gift, considering how hectic our lives are. Without her support at every turn, I'd never have completed it.

I also wish to thank Jayne Richards who magically entered our lives this past summer and re-invigorated this project in three substantial ways: first, she conducted the final editorial review; second, she was a substantial help in creating the initial cover design; and third, it was she who suggested "BDSM Mastery" as the series title. This project could not have reached such a successful conclusion without her friendship, hard work, and support

I should like to recognize a few people in particular who have either given me particularly useful insights or permitted me to reprint here some of the ideas that they, themselves, have developed. In alphabetical order, this includes:

- Chris_M (a serious thinker and writer about things ethical);
- Geoff W. (Evil_Geoff);

- Gloria McCauley (Executive Director, Buckeye region Anti-Violence Organization,
- Jay Wiseman (author of SM-101);
- lunaKM (owner of SubmissiveGuide.com);
- Maître Pierre and Mistress Catharine (owners of www.BDSMCircle.net);
- Master Arach (who blogs as TheEroticist.com);
- Master JW (an absolutely inspirational original thinker about Master/slave issues);
- Sabrina Santiago, MSW, (in collaboration with The Network/La Red www.tnlr.org and The New England Leather Alliance); and
- Sir Real (Atlanta, GA).

I also thank the many event producers over the years that have invited me to present at their conferences, concurrently exposing me to most of the best thinkers in this field. This book has benefited from that exposure and resulting cross-pollination of ideas.

Supplement E: About the authors

Robert J. Rubel, Ph. D.

Robert Rubel (Dr. Bob), author, educator and photographer is an educational sociologist and researcher by training. He currently has 10 books in print and two DVDs (Books: four on Master/slave topics, two on advanced sex techniques, one on fire play, and three erotic art photo books. DVDs: fire play and beginning impact play).

The recipient of the 2008 Pantheon of Leather's Community Choice Award (man), Dr. Bob has been involved in the BDSM and Total Power Exchange (TPE) scene since the summer of 2001, throwing himself into the literature of the field as though it were an academic study. He presents, judges, and sells his books at weekend kink conferences throughout the year.

Now starting his 70s, Bob has had three long-term relationships: a 17-year marriage, a 14-year marriage, and a 10-year Owner/property relationship in which after two years, his then-Owner gave him his own slave. The three of them remained together for eight more years. In his current relationship (that began early in 2010) Dr. Bob serves Jen, who is his Master and Owner.

Publications

Other Books published by Red Eight-Ball Press:

- *BDSM Mastery—Relationships: a guide for creating mindful relationships for Dominants and submissives.* (Rubel and Fairfield, 2014)
- *Master/slave Mastery: Updated handbook of concepts, approaches, and practices. (Rubel and Fairfield, 2015)*
- *Master/slave Mastery—Advanced: Refining the Fire--ideas that matter. (Rubel and Fairfield, 2015)*

- *Master/slave   Master—-Protocols: Focusing the intent of your relationship.* (Rubel and Fairfield, 2016)
- *Is THAT what they meant? A book of practical communication insights.* (Rubel and Fairfield, 2016)

Books Other BDSM Topics

- *Flames of Passion: Handbook of Erotic Fire Play.* Las Vegas: Nazca Plains, 2006.

SMTech Book+DVD Combinations

- *Fire Play: A Safety Training Course* (70-minute DVD plus 48-page book) Las Vegas: Nazca Plains, 2012
- *Impact Play 101: Building Your Skills* (70-minute DVD plus 48-page book) Las Vegas: Nazca Plains, 2012

Books on Advanced Sexual Practices

- *Squirms, Screams, and Squirts: Handbook for going from great sex to extraordinary sex.* Las Vegas: Nazca Plains, 2007.
- *Squirms, Screams, and Squirts: The Workbook.* Las Vegas: Nazca Plains, 2010.
- *Screams of Pleasure: Guide for Extraordinary Sex for those with Erectile Dysfunction* (Slightly revised version of Squirms, Screams, and Squirts) (2009)

Books of Erotic and Fetish Art

Three books on erotic and fetish photography titled (with an eye towards perverse humor):

- *Parts: The Erotic Photographic Art of Robert J. Rubel, PhD.* Las Vegas: Nazca Plains, 2006.
- *Wholes: The Erotic Photographic Art of Robert J. Rubel, PhD.* Las Vegas: Nazca Plains, 2006.
- *Holes: The Erotic Photographic Art of Robert J. Rubel,*

PhD. Las Vegas: Nazca Plains, 2006.

Edited Publications

Bob served as the Managing Editor of ***Power Exchange Magazine*** in 2007–2008. Issue Themes

- Master/slave Relations — male Master
- Master/slave Relations — female Master
- Bootblacking
- FemDomme
- Pony Play
- Polyamory
- Daddy/boy
- Leather Spirituality
- Pup/Trainer

In 2007 Bob made a marketing decision and transformed *Power Exchange Magazine* into a small book format. This series, *Power Exchange Books' Resource Series*, are 100-page books on focused topics of interest to BDSM or Leather folk. The series is about the *why* of what we do, not the *how* of it. Book titles include:

- *Playing with Disabilities*
- *The Art of Slavery*
- *Protocols: A Variety of Views*
- *Rope, Bondage, and Power*
- *Age Play*

M. Jen Fairfield

Jen is Dr. Bob's Master. She has extensive experience managing authority-imbalanced relationships. Her D/s experience began in 1992 as she dipped her toe in the water with a nurturing Mommy/boy relationship. Seeking more control than the Mommy/boy relationship could offer, Jen ended that relationship after a year and—following a year of introspection and personal clarification—entered a full-blown D/s relationship that she ran for another 16 years.

Jen found her home in the Leather Master/slave culture in the fall of 2010 and has embraced her calling as a Leather woman—to live a mindful and purpose-driven life with a partner (or partners) who are willing to hold themselves to exacting moral and ethical standards.

Jen has been attending conferences and workshops, reading books, and working closely with Dr. Bob as he has been researching and writing books and making presentations all over the U.S. and Canada. Over the last year, Jen has developed a growing number of presentations that are separate from Bob's.

Currently, Jen and Dr. Bob have books at various points of completion. At this point, their working titles are:

- *Master/slave Mastery—Hosting and Serving a High-Protocol Dinner.*
- *BDSM Mastery—Tradecraft: play skills and what you have to know about them.*
- *Master/slave Mastery—Repairing relationships/s with Intent*
- *BDSM Mastery—Sex: your guide for erotically adventuresome nights*

Made in the USA
Las Vegas, NV
16 January 2024

84461388R00134